PRAISE

for Spiritual Breakthrough

Elmer Towns has taught all the students at Liberty University and Liberty Baptist Theological Seminary to fast the way the Bible teaches. I fully recommend *The Daniel Fast for Spiritual Breakthrough* when you need God to answer a specific prayer.

Dr. Ergun Caner
President, Liberty Baptist Theological Seminary and Graduate School
Lynchburg, Virginia

When we were building our new facility in 2007, our staff committed to a 21-day Daniel Fast. We had a target date of March 2008 to be in our building. We knew that was a stretch, but we believed God for that date. During our fast, we discovered that the building crews were well ahead of schedule and we would actually celebrate Christmas 2007 in our new facility. God showed up in a big way, and 1,000 people were added to our services when we moved in. We believe it was a direct result of our focused prayer and fasting that God was able to do what even the construction crews could not explain. We have since made it a practice to do an annual fast, and we encourage our congregation to join with us.

Matt Fry
Lead Pastor of C3 Church, Clayton, North Carolina

This book is meant for this moment! The Holy Spirit is calling each believer to lay hold of the *power of fasting with prayer!* Daniel's prayer and fasting literally affected a shaping of history at a desperate time in the ancient world. Today, we are at a profound, prophetic intersection in time—one calling us to lay hold of the practical guidelines unfolded in this book. *The Daniel Fast for Spiritual Breakthrough* shows how God's people can see the same results in our generation but on Jesus' terms: "This kind can come out by nothing but prayer and fasting" (Mark 9:29).

Dr. Jack W. Hayford
Chancellor, The King's College and Seminary
Founding Pastor, The Church On The Way

When our church was having difficulty getting a building permit for its present worship sanctuary, Dr. Towns came and taught a seminar on fasting. Then we as a congregation fasted to intervene in what seemed like an "immovable mountain." God turned around an impossible situation, and we now are using that building to reach our community with the love and message of Jesus Christ. *The Daniel Fast for Spiritual Breakthrough* is a great spiritual tool for the work of the Kingdom.

Tom Mullins
Senior Pastor, Christ Fellowship, Palm Beach Gardens, Florida

Elmer Towns has been a friend of mine since the early 1970s and has made a contribution to my church both in Sunday school growth and the enrichment of prayer ministry. I've had him preach at pastoral conferences at my church on fasting and, in my opinion, he is a modern-day expert on fasting. The stories he tells in this book about how I led my church in a Daniel Fast indicate our commitment to fasting and prayer. Fasting remains a regular discipline among many of our people . . . and is part of my life.

Ron Phillips
Senior Pastor, Abba's House, Chattanooga, Tennessee

About two years after entering full-time ministry, I heard Dr. Towns speak on the power of fasting. Sadly, fasting was not part of my "Christian discipleship" process until that point. Since then, I have sought to incorporate fasting in my regular disciplines and into my church leadership, and I have experienced the spiritual power of fasting each time. This book is perfect for a personal or church-wide fast, and the daily readings will be an ever-present encouragement to you as you experience God's blessings through a planned season of fasting.

Nelson Searcy
Lead Pastor, The Journey Church (New York City)
Founder, ChurchLeaderInsights.com

Elmer Towns is a man who breathes with God! His insights come as if from heaven itself. Every ounce of this book is as powerful as a pound of dynamite! Elmer previously wrote a bestselling book on fasting, and now he has added even more to our spiritual arsenal. This book taught me something I did not know: targeted fasting, and how to aim for and hit a bull's eye in the spirit. Ready! Aim! Fast!

Tommy Tenney
Founder and CEO of GodChasers.network
Pineville, Louisiana

The DANIEL FAST

for Spiritual Breakthrough

ELMER L. TOWNS

Regal

From Gospel Light
Ventura, California, U.S.A.

Published by Regal
From Gospel Light
Ventura, California, U.S.A.
www.regalbooks.com
Printed in the U.S.A.

All Scripture quotations, unless otherwise indicated, are taken from the *New King James Version*.
Copyright © 1979, 1980, 1982 by Thomas Nelson, Inc. Used by permission. All rights reserved.

Other versions used are
CEV—*Contemporary English Version*. Copyright © American Bible Society, 1995.
Complete Jewish Bible—Copyright 1998 by David H. Stern. Published by Jewish New Testament Publications,
Inc. Distributed by Messianic Jewish Resources Int'l. All rights reserved. Used by permission.
CSB—*Holman Christian Standard Bible*. © 2001, Broadman and Holman Publishers, Lifeway Christian
Resources, 127 Ninth Avenue North, Nashville, TN 37234.
ELT—Scripture quotations marked ELT represent the author's paraphrase of Scripture.
KJV—*King James Version*. Authorized King James Version.
THE MESSAGE—Scripture taken from *THE MESSAGE*. Copyright © by Eugene H. Peterson, 1993, 1994,
1995. Used by permission of NavPress Publishing Group.
NASB—Scripture taken from the *New American Standard Bible,* © 1960, 1962, 1963, 1968, 1971, 1972, 1973,
1975, 1977, 1995 by The Lockman Foundation. Used by permission.
NET—Quotations designated (NET) are from The NET Bible® Copyright© 2005 by Biblical Studies Press,
L.L.C. www.bible.org. All Rights Reserved. Scripture quoted by permission.
NIV—Scripture taken from the *Holy Bible, New International Version®*. Copyright © 1973, 1978, 1984 by
International Bible Society. Used by permission of Zondervan Publishing House. All rights reserved.
NLT—Scripture quotations marked *NLT* are taken from the *Holy Bible, New Living Translation*, copyright ©
1996. Used by permission of Tyndale House Publishers, Inc., Wheaton, Illinois 60189. All rights reserved.
Phillips—*The New Testament in Modern English*, Revised Edition, J. B. Phillips, Translator. © J. B. Phillips 1958, 1960,
1972. Used by permission of Macmillan Publishing Co., Inc., 866 Third Avenue, New York, NY 10022.
TEV—Scripture quotations are from *Today's English Version*. Copyright © American Bible Society 1966, 1971,
1976. Used by permission.
TLB—Scripture quotations marked *(TLB)* are taken from *The Living Bible,* copyright © 1971.
Used by permission of Tyndale House Publishers, Inc., Wheaton, IL 60189. All rights reserved.

© 2010 Elmer L. Towns
All rights reserved.

Note: The fasts suggested in this book are not for everyone. Consult your physician before beginning.
Expectant mothers, diabetics, and others with a history of medical problems can enter the spirit of fasting
while remaining on essential diets. While fasting is healthful to many, the nature of God would not command a physical exercise that would harm people physically or emotionally.

Library of Congress Cataloging-in-Publication Data
Towns, Elmer L.
The Daniel fast for spiritual breakthrough / Elmer L. Towns.
p. cm.
ISBN 978-0-8307-5473-1 (trade paper)
1. Fasting—Religious aspects—Christianity. 2. Spiritual life—Christianity.
3. Bible. O.T. Daniel—Criticism, interpretation, etc. I. Title.
BV5055.T687 2010
248.4'7—dc22
2009046381

Fas

Rights for publishing this book outside the U.S.A. or in non-English languages are administered
by Gospel Light Worldwide, an international not-for-profit ministry. For additional information, please visit
www.glww.org, email info@glww.org, or write to Gospel Light Worldwide,
1957 Eastman Avenue, Ventura, CA 93003, U.S.A.

Dedicated to the memory of Jerry Falwell, my pastor,
who challenged me to my first day of fasting; and to Bill Bright,
who motivated me to my first 40-day fast. Also dedicated to
David Yonggi Cho, pastor of the world's largest church,
who challenged me to teach the ministerial students at Liberty
University to fast before seeking their first pastorate.

❈ Contents ❈

SECTION 3

APPENDICES

*Is this not the fast that I have chosen: To loose the bonds of wickedness,
to undo the heavy burdens, to let the oppressed go free, and that you break
every yoke? Is it not to share your bread with the hungry, and that you
bring to your house the poor who are cast out; when you see the naked,
that you cover him, and not hide yourself from your own flesh?
Then your light shall break forth like the morning, your healing shall
spring forth speedily, and your righteousness shall go before you;
the glory of the* LORD *shall be your rear guard.*

ISAIAH 58:6-8

The Impact of a Daniel Fast

In January 1998, our church entered into our Daniel Fast in the first three weeks of January. We had begun this practice several years before and had begun a cycle of harvest and multiplication in small groups.

It was on the fifteenth day of this fast that my wife and I were leaving Baton Rouge on the way to San Antonio to minister. As we drove around the curve where the governor's mansion is visible, in my spirit I saw a wind blow the door open (a brief mental image of this flashed across my mind as I looked over at the mansion). I told Melanie, my wife, "I believe God is about to open a door to the governor's mansion for a Bible study."

We ended the twenty-first day of the fast in San Antonio and returned to Baton Rouge. There, on my desk, was a note that the governor's secretary had called. When we returned her call, she told us that the governor had been exercising on his treadmill one week before when a daily 90-second program I have done for years came on the local affiliate. A voice inside of the governor said to him, "Call and ask this man to come teach you the entire Bible in four lessons."

This invitation was especially amazing because I had never met the governor before. On the appointed day, he was gathered with 15 of his top staff for the occasion. I taught them four Bible lessons: "creation," "chosen people," "Christ" and "the Church." At the end of the month, the governor asked that I continue. The Bible study continued through the remainder of his term and four additional years after his re-election! Many times I was able to pray with this group for miracles that stopped hurricanes, broke drought over the state, and brought great favor to this governor. He became the most popular governor our state has had in recent times before his retirement in 2004.

I am persuaded that this mighty open door came through the power of prayer and fasting. Even as Daniel himself prayed and fasted, God opened the doors to the highest levels of government and authority. After Paul's fast in Antioch (see Acts 13), God opened the door to the highest official in Cyprus, Sergius Paulus. Only the power of the Daniel Fast can bring a breakthrough in the United States and state governments, and my experience with the Governor of Louisiana is living proof of that reality.

Larry Stockstill
Senior Pastor, Bethany World Prayer Center
Baker, Louisiana

❧ INVITATION ❧

Welcome to *The Daniel Fast for Spiritual Breakthrough*. This book was written as a guide for your fast. You'll read an explanation of how the Daniel Fast was named, why it's either 10 or 21 days, what you should eat and how you should discipline yourself in a fast.

This book will also examine some of your prayer experiences while fasting. Perhaps you've committed to pray throughout the 10 or 21 days of your fast and, at the same time, fast for a prayer goal. You'll learn many practical tips on prayer. You'll learn how to encounter God, worship God and pray specifically for answers. You'll look at the role of weeping, repenting and what it means to crucify yourself. Then you'll learn some principles of warfare prayer and what it means to pray desperately.

If this is your first time ever to fast, this book will relieve some of your fears and explain some of the things you are experiencing while fasting. So read to get confidence in prayer and overcome anxiety; but most of all, read to get answers to your prayers.

As I wrote this book, I fasted several times, in several different ways. I was fasting and praying that God would show me what to write and help me prepare this book so that you would touch God as you read and fast; but more importantly, that God would touch you.

Written from my home at the
foot of the Blue Ridge Mountains,
Elmer L. Towns, 2009

About the Daniel Fast

❧ 1 ❧

What Is Fasting?

I was told that no one had written a bestselling book on fasting in 100 years, so when I wrote *Fasting for Spiritual Breakthrough* in 1996, I wanted some feedback. I mailed a typed copy of the manuscript to Pastor Ron Phillips of Central Baptist Church in greater Chattanooga, Tennessee. A few days later, I received a strange phone call.

"You're a dirty dog," the voice on the line said.

"Who's calling me a dirty dog?" I asked.

"This is Ron Phillips," he said with a laugh. Ron was a friend of mine; I had been to his church two or three times to hold Sunday School growth campaigns. "I'm at the Southern Baptist Convention," he went on, explaining his joking remark. "I should be attending meetings . . . and voting . . . and talking to my buddies down in the hallways, but I'm glued to this hotel room reading your book. This book is so good that it will change my life."

Before the phone call was over, Ron convinced me to come to his church to teach a Saturday seminar on the principles of fasting. So we set a date, and Ron sent out the invitations. He expected that 800 people would attend, but only 157 showed up. The reason for the lower attendance was because Ron had asked them to come and *fast* that day. Many people were scared away because they didn't know how to fast or didn't understand what God could do for them if they fasted. That convinced me that more needed to be written on fasting—whether it was a bestseller or not.

So, what does it mean to "fast"?

Definition

Fast (fa:st, -æ-): To abstain from food, or to restrict oneself to
a meager diet, either as a religious observance or as a ceremonial
expression of grief; to go without food; also (contextually)
to go without drink; to pass (time) fasting; to keep or observe
(a day, etc.) as a time of abstinence.[1]

God created the human body to require food to keep it oper-
ating. To make sure the body gets fuel, God created within us an
appetite for food, called hunger. Eating satisfies our appetite and
gives us the strength to do the activities we need to do throughout
our day. So why would a person choose to fast—to go without food
for a period of time?

From God's perspective, the reason is simple. Fasting can be
used to accomplish a spiritual purpose. In the Old Testament, the
Israelites were commanded to fast once each year: "In the seventh
month, on the tenth day, you shall go without eating" (Lev. 16:29,
CEV). This fast took place on the Day of Atonement (Yom Kippur). On this day, the high priest would conduct special sacrifices
to atone for the sins of the people. During the service, the high
priest entered into the Holy of Holies in the center of the Temple—
the only time of the year that he was allowed inside. God wanted
His people to fast on this day in order to remember the experience
of their salvation. Eveyone fasted in order to identify with the high
priest, who sacrificed a lamb for the forgiveness of their sins.

Today, as Christians we live under grace, so we are no longer *required* to fast. However, Jesus makes it clear in Matthew 6:16 that
we are *allowed* to fast for certain reasons: "Moreover, when you fast,
do not be like the hypocrites, with a sad countenance. For they dis-
figure their faces that they may appear to men to be fasting. Assuredly, I say to you, they have their reward." Likewise, in Matthew
9:15, He states, "Can the friends of the bridegroom mourn as long
as the bridegroom is with them? But the days will come when the
bridegroom will be taken away from them, and then they will fast."
We also see the apostles in the Early Church fasting for a spiritual
purpose: "As they ministered to the Lord and fasted, the Holy

Spirit said, 'Now separate to Me Barnabas and Saul for the work to which I have called them.' Then, having fasted and prayed, and laid hands on them, they sent them away" (Acts 13:2-3).

Many people who have never fasted before get nervous about the prospects of abstaining from food. They wonder if they will get hungry and if the hunger pains will make it too difficult for them to continue. They anticipate that it will be an unpleasant experience—probably many of the same concerns that the members of Central Baptist Church felt when Ron Phillips asked them to fast. However, keep in mind that fasting will not hurt any more than dieting to get thinner. It will also not harm you; in fact, some studies show fasting is actually good for the body, as it eliminates toxins from the body.

The purpose of fasting is not to make an outward show of your religious dedication to God, but rather to make a personal commitment between you and God. It's not always easy—like any spiritual discipline, you will undoubtedly encounter resistance and opposition. So embark on your Daniel Fast—or any fast you undertake—with the full understanding of what you are doing. Know also that although the path may be difficult, the rewards will be great.[2]

My Time to Pray

Lord, I pray that You will guide me as I begin this time of fasting.
AMEN.

Notes

1. See http://dictionary.oed.com/cgi/entry/50082578?query_type=word&queryword=fast&first=1&max_to_show=10&sort_type=alpha&search_id=ydSC-7mmrRh-7573&result_place=1, s.v. "fast" (accessed July 1, 2009).
2. For a further explanation of the purpose of fasting, see *The Beginner's Guide to Fasting* (Ventura, CA: Regal, 2001), pp. 9-15.

What Is a Daniel Fast?

Jentezen Franklin, pastor of the Free Chapel in Gainesville, Georgia—a congregation with 10,000 in attendance—begins each year with a 21-day Daniel Fast. Everyone participates in some measure. Some people in the church fast for one day, others for three days, some for one week, and many for the full 21 days. Jentezen has said, "I've had people testify that only three days into a fast for a loved one suffering from cancer, the cancer was completely cured at this point. Another lady's son was dying from 107-degree fever, associated with his leukemia. The very first day of the fast the boy's fever broke and he didn't suffer a trace of brain damage!"[1]

Jentezen believes it is important in the spiritual growth of the congregation at Free Chapel to fast and sacrifice for God at the beginning of every new year. Some fast to break their addiction to junk food, some fast to break the power of an uncontrollable appetite, and some fast to break addiction to nicotine, alcohol or drugs, but most fast to know God intimately. Jentezen Franklin has said, "Each year I encourage all the members of Free Chapel to join us in our 21-day fast. If in 21 days you can be a new person, why go the rest of your life feeling sick, weak, overweight, and run down? Why not take a radical step of faith? We have only one life to give God—let's get control of our bodies and go for God with the best we have!"[2]

So, how did Daniel get a fast named after him? In other words, why did Daniel fast? Daniel was 16 years old when the Babylonians took him captive. At that time, the king of Babylon was Nebuchadnezzar. Daniel had served in the king's court in Jerusalem, so he was being prepared for some type of government service in Babylon. Nebuchadnezzar chose Daniel because he wanted "young men in whom *there was* no blemish, but good-looking, gifted in all wisdom, possessing knowledge and quick to understand" (Dan. 1:4, emphasis added).

Nebuchadnezzar wanted Daniel "to serve in the king's palace" (v. 4) and help him administer his rule over the Jews, God's people. But he wanted Daniel to be "Babylonian." So, "the king appointed for them [Daniel and three of his friends] a daily provision of the king's delicacies and of the wine which he drank" (v. 5).

To a teenager today, the word "delicacies" means foods like pizza or ice cream . . . and he or she might also include beer and alcohol—and even drugs—to the list. But Daniel didn't choose luxuries; rather, "Daniel purposed in his heart that he would not defile himself with the portion of the king's delicacies, nor with the wine" (v. 8). Notice the word "purposed" in this passage. The secret to a Daniel Fast is to *purpose* in your heart; that is, to make a vow as you enter the fast that you will purpose to follow the Lord in what you eat and drink.

What did Daniel choose to eat? The *King James Version* of the Bible says that Daniel told his supervisor, "Prove thy servants, I beseech thee, ten days; and let them give us *pulse* to eat, and water to drink" (v. 12, emphasis added). The newer translations use the word "vegetables" for "pulse," which were probably leafy vegetables such as lettuce, turnip greens, cabbage, spinach and collard greens. So, Daniel ate a "salad" diet. What were the results? "At the end of ten days their features appeared better and fatter in flesh than all the young men who ate the portion of the king's delicacies" (v. 15).

The test that Daniel proposed to his supervisor appears to be a simple one, and as you enter the Daniel Fast, you may choose to eat only vegetables for 10 days. However, you may also choose to partake in a longer version of the Daniel Fast, as recorded in chapter 10: "I ate no pleasant food, no meat or wine came into my mouth" (v. 3). Daniel continued with this fast for 21 days, "till three whole weeks were fulfilled" (v. 3).

The phrase "pleasant food" is interesting in this passage. "Pleasant food" means food that you would consider pleasant to your taste, such as steak, clam chowder, fried shrimp, escargot, veal cutlets with provolone, and so on. The *NIV* translates it "choice food," the *CEV* calls it "fancy food," the *CSB* and *TLB* translate it "rich food," the *Complete Jewish Bible* translates the phrase "only food that satisfies me," and *The Companion Bible* translates it "bread of desires." All of these definitions point to the same issue: During a Daniel Fast, you give up the things you enjoy eating and eat only what is necessary. Therefore, the Daniel Fast is an expression of abstinence for purposes of self-discipline.

My Time to Pray
Lord, I purpose to follow You in what I eat and drink.
AMEN.

Notes
1. Jentezen Franklin, *Fasting: Opening the Door to a Deeper, More Intimate, More Powerful Relationship with God* (Lake Mary, FL: Charisma House, 2008), p. 55.
2. Ibid., p. 42.

Why Choose to Fast?

Daniel and his three friends were put through a Babylonian "training program" to prepare them to become managers of programs for a foreign government. Part of the Babylonians' religion was a special diet, so the young men were immersed in Babylonian customs, laws, values and beliefs.

Daniel and his friends asked to be excused from eating the meat and drinking the wine. Perhaps this was because the food was offered to idols, and eating it would have compromised their separation from false gods. Perhaps the wine was intoxicating, which would have violated their Jewish practice. Or perhaps the food included non-kosher meat, which would have violated the Jewish dietary laws. Whatever the cause, Daniel knew the king's food was off limits to him and his three friends.

So Daniel purposed in his heart that he would not defile himself with the portion of the king's delicacies (see Dan. 1:8). Was this a choice for good health, or to keep his body separated to God? It was both! Daniel wanted God's will for his body. And isn't that what you want for your body, too, during your Daniel Fast?

The Daniel Fast is not primarily a dietary choice; it is a *spiritual vow* to God. You may lose weight during your fast, or you may lower your blood pressure or cholesterol, and while these results are good, they are not the primary focus of the fast. Instead, you are fasting for a *spiritual focus*. Improved health is always a *secondary* result of doing the Daniel Fast. Look at what happens when you begin a Daniel Fast. First, you reevaluate your life in light of

God's perspective. Second, you break some bad eating habits, which will begin to restore you to better health. If you join with your church or other Christian group as you do the Daniel Fast to pray for a spiritual goal, you also build up your self-control. The outward accountability you gain in doing the fast with others will strengthen your self-discipline.

When you begin a Daniel Fast, you also begin the process of purifying your body from fats and perhaps other negative side effects that come from eating meat. You repent of sin (probably not the sin of eating meat, but other sins associated with the flesh) and are drawn closer to God through the experience. In fact, many people who participate in a Daniel Fast testify that they are closer to God when they fast than any other time in their life. Why? Because they are obeying God *every minute of the day*. When you're fasting, you're aware of your stomach all the time, which makes you aware of the reason you are abstaining from food—intimacy with God—as you fast.

A final reason to choose to fast is that it leads to worshiping God. When you fast and pray, you honor the Lord with your body *and* soul.

My Time to Pray
Lord, be glorified in my body during my Daniel Fast.
AMEN.

❧ 4 ❧

Why Vow?

The Daniel Fast is a *lengthy vow*; it is longer than a one-day fast (such as the Yom Kippur Fast, in which Jewish people traditionally fast for a 24-hour period). As we previously noted, Daniel and his young friends fasted for 10 days (see Dan. 1), and then later, Daniel fasted for 21 days (see Dan. 11).

Regardless of whether you are fasting for 10 days or for 21 days, the two questions you should be asking yourself are the same: (1) *Why am I fasting?* and (2) *What do I want to accomplish with this fast?* Technically, you should be fasting for focus and commitment to a project or for an answer to prayer. In this Daniel Fast, you've made a vow of abstinence to get the answer from God you seek. You've vowed to fast and pray for an answer from God.

The Daniel Fast is a *time vow*, so you need to decide ahead of time how long you will fast and then be firm to that commitment to the end. Because I've written several books on fasting, I receive letters from people who tell me about their experiences with fasting. On occasion, some individuals will tell me that they are on the forty-second day of a 40-day fast and are enjoying the experience so much that they don't want to stop. They ask, "What should I do?" I write back and tell them to stop immediately. Their fast was a *time vow*. They should begin on time, keep the promise to fast the entire time, and end on time.

The Daniel Fast is also a *discipline vow*. You strengthen your character in every area of your life when you fulfill your Daniel Fast. When you take control of your body—your outer self—you begin to take control of your inner character. You discipline your body to glorify the Lord.

The Daniel Fast is a *spiritual commitment*. You pray while fasting for a *spiritual goal*. Remember, fasting will not accomplish much without serious, sacrificial prayer. As you discipline your body, you are disciplining your prayer life.

The Daniel Fast is a *faith vow*. In Mark 11:22, Jesus exhorted His disciples, "Have faith in God." To explain how they could express their faith, He directed them, "Whoever says to this mountain [problem or goal], 'Be removed and be cast into the sea,' and does not doubt in his heart, but believes that those things he says will be done, he will have whatever he says" (v. 23). When Daniel began his fast, he made a statement of faith to eat only vegetables and drink water. Likewise, your fast is a verbal statement of what you want God to do.

The Daniel Fast is a *partial vow*. You don't give up all food (an absolute fast), nor do you go on just a juice fast (a normal fast). Instead, you omit certain foods that you would typically eat or eliminate certain meals for a specified period of time. This may include omitting one or two meals a day for a certain length of time, or it may involve omitting other practices.

The Daniel Fast is a *healthy vow*. You abstain from "party" food, or junk food. Usually, you don't eat between meals, and you only eat healthy foods.

Finally, the Daniel Fast is a *lifestyle vow*. When Daniel asked permission to avoid the king's delicacies for 10 days, he put his whole life into his chosen diet. Then, if he continued to look "healthy," he could continue following his own diet.

Some who take a vow against alcoholic beverages take a lifelong vow—they commit to never taste alcoholic drinks again. They may make this vow for health reasons, because alcohol consumption can lead to cirrhosis of the liver and premature death. Some people make the vow because of addiction to alcohol—they have been a slave to it. Still others vow not to taste alcohol for spiritual reasons, because they believe drinking alcohol is wrong. (My father died an alcoholic, and my family suffered poverty and other problems because of his addiction. I have read the Scriptures closely and personally I conclude that drinking in any form is wrong.) In the Bible, John the Baptist, the prophet Samuel, and Samson made lifelong vows to avoid alcohol. If we want to honor the Lord as they did, we should follow their example in their Nazirite vow (see Num. 6:1-8).

Take note that nowhere in the Bible are believers commanded to observe a Daniel Fast. We have been given freedom to eat; and we eat healthy to stay healthy. God told Peter, "Rise, Peter; kill and eat" (Acts 10:13), thereby discontinuing ceremonial laws. So whenever you eat good food, eat with a good conscience to the glory of God. "Whatever you do, do it heartily, as to the Lord" (Col. 3:23). But still, some will feel guilty when they end their Daniel Fast and return to their normal eating habits. But remember, in the Old Testament, God prescribed only one day for fasting (Yom Kippur or the Day of Atonement) but seven feast days. So God likes for His people to eat, enjoy their food and be happy.

Some food, however, is not good for you. America seems to be living in a day of epidemic obesity because some eat too much while others continually eat the wrong foods. This is why believers should pledge themselves to a lifelong Daniel lifestyle, not just a Daniel Fast. For the Daniel lifestyle is a healthy lifestyle: "At the end of ten days their features [Daniel and his three friends] appeared better and fatter in the flesh than all the young men who ate the portion of the King's delicacies" (Dan. 1:15). And this lifestyle leads to a clearer mind and better thinking: "The king interviewed them, and among them none was found like Daniel . . . and in all manners of wisdom *and* understanding about which the king examined them, he found them ten times better than all the magicians *and* astrologists" (Dan. 1:19-20).

My Time to Pray

Lord, I will fast for the entire length of my fast. I will keep the time period of my vow. I will discipline my physical body, and I will discipline my prayer life.

Lord, I will fast and pray for my goal. I give up pleasure to seek Your presence and pray for my goal. Strengthen my body as I fast.

Lord, I want You to be glorified in my body. I fast to obey Your Word, and I pray to worship You with my fast.

Lord, I will eat healthy food so that I will be healthy. Give me wisdom to choose healthy food and the discipline to stick to my choice. Protect me from germs, bacteria, poisons and toxins that could damage my health. Protect me when I can't protect myself.
AMEN.

What Can I Withhold?

In the first chapter, I told the story of how Ron Phillips, pastor of Central Baptist Church in greater Chattanooga, Tennessee, invited me to come to his church to teach a seminar on fasting. I taught the Saturday seminar from 9:00 A.M. to 3:00 P.M. When I finished, Ron jumped up in front of the people and excitedly said to them, "We've got to organize ourselves to pray. We are a typical Southern Baptist church that organizes everything but prayer."

Ron asked everyone to take a visitor's card out of the pew, fill it out, and promise to fast one day each month for the church. People reached into the pew rack to make a written vow. At least 123 members signed up.

Ron continued his motivation. "We just had a revival meeting this week—Sunday through Wednesday—but not much happened. There were 12 decisions at the altar, and some of those were just children getting ready to be baptized." Ron spoke of desiring a congregation-shaking revival that came by prayer and fasting. He appointed a lady on the spot to be the prayer coordinator to organize the people so there would be one person "covering the church" every day of each month by fasting and prayer. He also assigned several people to cover the church each Sunday with fasting and prayer.

Ron's preaching took on a decidedly "spiritual" nature as a result of that conference. He called the church to sincere prayer and fasting. A few months later, another evangelistic campaign was held, and there were 998 decisions at the altar. Sunday School attendance jumped to 258, Sunday worship attendance jumped to 401, and the church received approximately $500,000 more that month than in the same month the previous year. Fasting and prayer works.

God honored the church's spiritual commitment. Two years later, the church was bulging at the seams. They now had three worship services and needed desperately to build larger facilities. So during one service, Ron passed out a card and asked the people to enter a 40-day fast with him, the deacons and the church staff. The idea of a 40-day fast scared most of the congregation. Ron smiled and told them it was a different kind of fast. He was suggesting a Daniel Fast.

Ron held up a card and asked each member to read the four prayer requests printed on the front. The first request was to pray for the size of the new auditorium. The present sanctuary seated 600, so Ron asked the people to pray whether they should build 1,200 seats, 2,400 seats, 3,600 seats, or 4,800 seats. "The decision is not ours; it's God's decision," he said. "Let's find His will by fasting and prayer."

The second request was about the type of sanctuary they should build. Ron asked them to fast and pray about whether they should build a traditional Southern Baptist sanctuary or a performing arts auditorium like those found in a civic center, so the church could have television productions, musicals and various activities.

The third request was about the location of their property. God had given the church a large piece of property that stretched from one major highway to another, around the back of businesses. He challenged the congregation, "Let's make the decision where to locate the new bulding by prayer and fasting."

The fourth request was for finances. They would need money equal to the size of their vision.

Ron then turned the card over to reveal several ways the people could fast for the items they wanted from God. "I'm going to explain the importance of each activity," he announced, "and then ask you to make a 40-day vow to fast and pray in just one of these ways for the spiritual future of the church." These are the guidelines he explained to his congregation:

- *One meal each day.* The fast is not about only giving up food, but also includes praying during a mealtime. Jesus said, "Could you not watch with Me one hour?" (Matt. 26:40). It takes about an hour to prepare a meal or travel to a restaurant or get ready to eat, so this time is a perfect opportunity to pray. Those who work in hot, exhausting jobs cannot fast completely because they need their strength and stamina for physical exertion, but they can sacrifice one meal a day for God.

- *Two meals each day.* Some people can pray for two hours each day, sacrificing two meals to God.

- *Eat only vegetables.* The Daniel Fast involves giving up meats, desserts and snacks, eating only the food that Daniel ate. While the fast doesn't give extra time to pray, it is a commitment of the heart that, when joined with prayer, moves the heart of God.

- *Give up television.* Secular folks might laugh at "fasting television"—sacrificing television—but it is a commitment to God to put Christ first. This is a spiritual choice in response to Christ, who promised, "Seek first the kingdom of God and His righteousness, and all these things shall be added to you" (Matt. 6:33).

- *Give up sports.* Giving up bowling, golfing, fishing, jogging or any other activity for 40 days to pray during that time is a choice to put spiritual exercise above physical exercise. "Bodily exercise profits little, but godliness is profitable for all things" (1 Tim. 4:8).

- *Give up pleasure reading.* Beyond required reading for a job or preparing Sunday School lessons at church, pleasure reading can be turned into prayer time. You could also give up newspaper reading for prayer.

- *Other.* This is a flexible area. Individuals can fast from anything that God brings to mind.

- *Vow.* This "faith commitment" requires the person to sign a card as a commitment to God, not to the church or to the pastor.

- *Restrict cell phone and text messaging activities.* While some use of these communication devices may be necessary, they are serious time-consuming factors to curtail during a Daniel Fast. (In the fourth quarter of 2008, teens text-messaged approximately an average of 2,272 text messages per month—almost 80 messages a day.[1])

- *Use of iPhone or MP3 players.* Some have restricted their listening of music to only Christian music during a Daniel Fast (praise worship music that prepares the heart for prayer). That means listening to no secular music during a Daniel Fast.

I was at the Metropolitan Church of God in Birmingham, Alabama, where Raymond Culpepper was pastor. (Today he is the head overseer of the Church of God, Cleveland, Tennessee.) His church was attempting to raise $5 million for a youth activity building. The audience of 2,000 people was asked to sign a vow card similar to the one used by Ron Phillips at Central Baptist Church. Pastor Culpepper said, "We will not collect the cards as we collect an offering each Sunday. I want you to come to the church altar, bow in prayer to commit yourself to the vow you are making, and then leave your card on the altar." So many people came to the altar that there was no space left. They knelt in the aisles, and then sailed their cards onto the platform. These people took their vows to pray literally.

What can be learned from these churches? Little things become big in God's sight when they are an expression of one's dedication to God. God takes note of small acts of our love: "Whenever you did this for one of the least important . . . you did it for me" (Matt. 25:40, *TEV*). So, remember, you are not primarily fasting for your church nor primarily to get an answer to prayer or for anything else. You are fasting to God, for you made your vow to Him. "God is not unjust to forget your work and labor of love which you have shown toward His name" (Heb. 6:10).

Daniel Fast Suggestions

Eliminate one meal a day and pray during that mealtime.

Eliminate two meals a day, and pray during their times.

Eliminate all desserts.

Eliminate all rich, superfluous foods eaten only for pleasure.

Eat only necessities, and only during mealtime (no snacks).

Eliminate all drinks except water
(no coffee, tea, soda or purchased drinks).

Contemporary Interpretations of the Daniel Fast

No text messaging or Facebook or Twitter communications that take your thoughts away from God.

No secular music; only praise and worship music.

No newspaper or pleasure reading; give that time to prayer.

No television; give that time to prayer.

No recreational sports; give that time to prayer.

No sex. "Both husband and wife to refrain from sexual intimacy for a limited time, so they can give themselves completely to prayer" (1 Cor. 7:5, *NLT*).

My Time to Pray

Lord, I dedicate small things to express the greatness of Your supremacy in all of life.

Lord, I will be faithful in little expressions of my faith for great answers to prayer.

Lord, I vow to fulfill these small expressions of my love to You.
AMEN.

Note

1. Katie Hafner, "Texting May Be Taking a Toll," *New York Times*, May 26, 2009, sec. Health. http://www.nytimes.com/2009/05/26/health/26teen.html?_r=2&em> (accessed June 10, 2009).

What Is the Primary Focus of the Daniel Fast?

As you enter the Daniel Fast, it is easy to focus on the food you give up or the activities you surrender. It's easy to focus on your abstinence and not on the basic purpose for which you are fasting. But remember that God is not impressed just because you stop eating altogether or you stop eating certain foods, even if you do it for your health. God is not impressed with the outward actions of your fast. The secret of any fast is not what you keep from entering the stomach but what comes out of the heart. God is primarily concerned with your inner person, not your outer body.

In Mark 9:29, Jesus described the spiritual energy needed to remove spiritual barriers: "This kind can come out by nothing but prayer and fasting." So, you must give yourself completely to prayer *and* to fasting. The commitment of your outer body to fasting reflects your inner commitment to prayer. Notice also that the phrase "prayer and fasting" in this verse emphasizes continuous action. This means that you should fast more than once or make fasting a continuous practice. During your Daniel Fast, your decision of what you eat or what you withhold will have more influence on your prayer life than most other spiritual exercises. If you're flippant with the Daniel Fast, you're likely to be flippant with your prayer dedication.

The basic principles of discipleship were not *denial* or *self-discipline*, but following Jesus Christ. Jesus said, "If any one desires to come after Me, let him deny himself, and take up his cross daily, and follow Me" (Luke 9:23). This involves turning to the Lord and putting Him first in your life, and then turning away from anything that keeps you from following Him.

There are three words in this verse that should influence your Daniel Fast. First, the word "deny" means that you should get rid of anything that hinders your relationship with Christ. You must get off of the throne of your heart, and Jesus must sit there and control what you eat and drink. The second word is "daily." Following Jesus means 24-7 dedication, so your Daniel Fast requires a 10-day or 21-day vow accompanied with continuous prayer. The third word is "follow." Just as Jesus fasted in preparation for His spiritual work, so must you follow Jesus' example with a Daniel Fast for your spiritual vow.

My Time to Pray

Lord, I will deny myself enjoyment during my Daniel Fast so that I can seek Your will in my life. I count it a privilege to give up my "pleasant food" for Your glory and as a commitment of my prayer.

Lord, I have made a spiritual vow to You that I will faithfully fast and pray for 10 days or 21 days.

Lord, give me strong outer discipline to keep my outer vow to You, and give me strong inner commitment to pray faithfully for the answer I seek.
AMEN.

How Can I Prepare for My Fast?

In 1971, when I moved to Lynchburg, Virginia, from Greater Chicago, Illinois, there was a downturn in the Chicago real estate market. So I continued to own my home there and make monthly payments on it. I moved into a house in Lynchburg and made monthly payments on that house as well. Each month I prayed for the sale of the Illinois house, but I wasn't praying with a lot of faith. I found it hard to be optimistic when the bottom had dropped out of the market. My eyes were on circumstances, not on God's ability to do the miraculous.

At one point, I said to my wife, "Let's fast together on the fifteenth day of the month for God to sell the Chicago house." The mortgage was due on the fifteenth, while my Lynchburg house payment was due on the first of the month. I had arranged it that way long before thinking about praying for God's intervention. That first month we fasted and prayed, but nothing happened. No word from Chicago. Then I completely forgot about fasting, even though I continued to pray each day for the house to sell.

As I got ready to write the next month's payment, I again said to my wife, "Let's fast together on the fifteenth for God to sell the house." We did, and again nothing happened. No word from Chicago.

I continued praying daily, and Ruth and I fasted on the fifteenth day of each succeeding month, even though nothing was happening. Then, after six months, our realtor called and said,

"Pray . . . I've got a hot one." He was a Christian friend, but I didn't tell him that we were fasting.

At the end of a year, I went to Chicago to sign closing papers for the sale. I was talking casually with the buyer when he mentioned that he had been looking at our house for about a year. He then gave me the exact date that he had first looked at our house, stating, "It was on my wife's birthday." It was the sixteenth day of the month after Ruth and I first prayed—the day after we fasted! The hair on my arms and the back of my neck bristled. *This is God's work*, I thought.

I learned three lessons about fasting and prayer from my first successful fast. First, *when daily prayer is not enough, fasting takes prayer to a higher level.* God knows your heart, but when you demonstrate your sincerity with fasting, God listens attentively and responds.

Second, *there is power in two or more people agreeing to pray and fast together.* Jesus taught, "Again I say to you that if two of you agree on earth concerning anything that they ask, it will be done for them by my Father in Heaven" (Matt. 18:19). So, there is power when you join together with your spouse, your church or with any other group of God's people to pray—especially when you set a goal and make a vow to fast together for that goal.

Third, *persistence is key.* Once you begin fasting, don't quit. I am afraid to think what would have happened if Ruth and I had quit when the house didn't sell the first time we fasted. Continuing to fast demonstrates your faithfulness to God and your belief that He will do something mighty—and that He will do it in answer to your prayer.

Now let's talk in more detail about your fast. As you approach fasting and prayer, there are three items to put in place. First, you need to have a *goal.* In my case, my goal was to sell a house. Second, you need to develop a *plan.* My plan was to fast each month on the fifteenth day of the month. Third, you need to make a *vow*—a promise to complete the fast.

You probably already have a project or goal in mind, but let me suggest that you use a Fasting Checklist similar to the one on the following page. Just as an airplane pilot will go through a checklist to make sure everything is perfect before he starts down the runway—knowing that if even one little item is overlooked, it could cause a

FASTING CHECKLIST

Aim: To sell my house in Greater Chicago.

Affirmation: I believe that God answers my prayer when I ask specifically in Jesus' name and when I meet the conditions of intercession. Therefore, I enter this Daniel Fast asking God to answer prayers for the vow for which I have committed myself.

What I will withhold: This will be a Yom Kippur Fast (i.e., a one-day fast).

Begin: Sundown on the 14th.

End: Sundown on the 15th.

When I will pray: The 15th day of each month.

Biblical basis: Matthew 18:19.

Bible promise: "Again, I tell you that if two of you on earth agree about anything you ask for, it will be done for you by my Father in heaven. For where two or three come together in my name, there am I with them" (Matt. 18:19, *NIV*).

Resources needed: I will write in my prayer journal what God tells me.

Prayer partner: My wife, Ruth.

Steps after fast: Prepare for a fast next month.

crash—so you should be equally diligent when you prepare for your journey. After all, your fast is just as important, if not more important. A pilot is dealing with temporal life, but you are dealing with *spiritual* life. So use the checklist, or make up your own checklist, to ensure that you have thought of everything and that you have all you need to begin your fast, and make copies so that you will have the checklist each time you fast. (The sample checklist on the previous page is based on my experience of fasting and praying for the house in 1972 and will give you an idea of what you can do to record your faith project.)

As you fill out your Fasting Checklist, there are six attitude preparations that will help you accomplish your faith goal. These are:

1. *Focus on your need.* You are going to do something that is not in your normal routine or inclination. You are choosing to not eat (or not participate in other activities) for a purpose. Focus on what you want God to do for you. Write the need exactly; it will help you focus what you are doing in your mind and bring out your sincerity to follow through.

2. *Focus on what you will do.* You are going to do something about the need. You are going to bring the problem to the Lord God of the universe. Focus on your prayer relationship with God to solve the problem.

3. *Begin and end with a purpose.* Some people find they have missed a meal and decide to call it a "fast." Just missing a meal because of circumstances is not a fast unless you purposed beforehand to pray and use the time of not eating for a spiritual purpose. God knows your heart. Also, don't enter into a fast with the idea of seeing how far you can go or how far you can hold out before you have to eat. Begin with purpose and end at the assigned time. Then begin on a specific date and end on a specific date. Finish strong! Then break your fast and eat in victory, with rejoicing.

4. *Gather the needed resources.* Before you begin your fast, gather resources that will be needed during the fast. If you're fasting for a person, get a picture of that person to hold during prayer and to heighten your memory. If you're fasting over bills, spread them out before you as you pray over them. Do the same if you're fasting about hiring or firing someone. Spread out the person's personnel records before you as you pray. Sometimes I select a spiritual book I want to read while fasting. Or it could be some DVD that I want to see or a CD that I want to hear.

5. *Remember the "inner journey principle."* Just as a person never takes a journey without first planning the journey within, so you must prepare yourself inwardly for a fast before you can be successful outwardly. In the same way that inner rings on a tree trunk tell of its growth, you will develop inner character as you control your outward diet.

6. *Make a vow.* Again, remember that fasting is a private vow that you make to God. Even if you are joining with others in your church in doing the fast (or even joining just one other person, such as your spouse), you must deal with the issue privately with God before you join with others.

Filling out a Fasting Checklist will help you think through all the aspects of what you are about to do. Note that you don't have to sign the vow, but I urge you to do so. When you sign a contract with the world, you are pledging yourself to others and what you will do along with them. When you fast with others, they are expecting you to do your part. So sign the checklist as a promise to God and to yourself. The vow says, "God, this is what I will do."

Now it's your turn. As you fill out your checklist for the fasting and prayer project that you are now doing or are considering doing, you may also want to refer to the appendices, as they provide helpful information about reasons for fasting, the various kinds of biblical fasts and practical help for your health in fasting. I recommend that you permanently keep your Fasting Checklist— a record of your faith journey. Hopefully, you will start a notebook of collecting many such documents as you continue to trust God and seek intimacy with Him throughout your lifetime.

My Time to Pray

Lord, I have a great need that I bring to You. Help me fast and pray for this need.

Lord, my faith is not always strong and does not always prevail. "I believe, help my unbelief" (Mark 9:24).

Lord, I vow to fast according to the Fasting Checklist. Help me keep to my vow, and please answer my prayer.
AMEN.

❧ SECTION 2 ❧

Daily Readings

WEEK ONE
Day 1 to Day 7 Overview

Learning About Fasting

A journey of 1,000 miles begins with the first step, and a 10- or 21-day fast begins on Day One. So approach the first day with obedience—praying as sincerely as you will on the last day.

Enter the first day with hope that God will answer and give you the faith project for which you pray.

Don't forget commitment. Determine that you will keep your vow to fast and pray until the end of your committed time. These daily readings are written to instruct you more fully in a Daniel Fast, as well as to motivate you daily to continue to the end.

This Daniel Fast may be the greatest step of faith you've ever taken in your life. May Christ be magnified in your prayer life, and may you experience deep spiritual growth through this fast.

Daily Readings

Day 1: Your Private Prayer in a Daniel Fast
Day 2: Joining Others in a Daniel Fast
Day 3: Daily Commitment During Your Fast
Day 4: Praying and Fasting for a Project
Day 5: Benefits of a Lengthy Fast
Day 6: Saying No in Prayer
Day 7: The Persistence of a Daniel Fast

 DAY 1

Your Private Prayer in a Daniel Fast

But you, when you fast, anoint your head and wash your face, so that you do not appear to men to be fasting, but to your Father who is in the secret place; and your Father who sees in secret will reward you openly.

MATTHEW 6:17-18

My granddaughter Beth heard me talking about fasting to the family. She knew I had a bestseller book—*Fasting for Spiritual Breakthrough*—that won the Silver Medallion (second place) for the Evangelical Christian Publishers Association. But I never asked her to fast, nor did I ever carry on a private conversation with her about fasting.

Need is what usually drives us to fasting, and that happened to Beth, a 12-year-old middle school student. Her youth group had a puppet team of which she was a member (she activated one puppet into life). They planned a trip to the juvenile detention center in our city to entertain and present the gospel through singing and puppet-enacted stories to young boys who had gotten into trouble.

No one told Beth to fast, but God put a burden on her heart to see God work through her group's presentation. Beth and her team members prayed together, but she decided to fast alone. She didn't even tell the others what she planned to do.

Beth decided on a one-day fast to pray that some of the detainees in the center would pray to receive Christ. She didn't tell me or tell her parents until she was already in the fast. She said, "Mother, I'm not going to eat this evening; I'm fasting for some guys to get saved when Power Source goes to the juvenile center."

How did Jesus describe a child's faith? He sat a child in the middle of His quarrelling disciples and said, "Of such is the kingdom of heaven" (Matt. 19:14). Read on to find how God honored Beth's faith.

On the afternoon of her fast, Beth ate a snack in her bedroom when she got home from school. She began her fast at sundown and only drank something for the evening meal in her room. She spent some time praying for the puppet presentation, and specifically for her part.

The next morning Beth didn't eat breakfast; she only drank a glass of orange juice (because her grandfather drinks orange juice in the morning when he's fasting). She prayed especially before going to school.

During lunch she got permission to remain in her homeroom and didn't go to the lunchroom. She told me, "All I could think about all afternoon was food."

Then in her youthful innocence she said, "I was glad when the sun went down so I could eat a snack before dinner."

God in heaven sees all the "simple" things we do for Him. While Beth's experience may sound simple to us, this was a huge step of faith for her. And doesn't God measure our step of faith by the maturing of our faith and then reward us accordingly?

So what was the result? Several of the boys prayed to receive Christ at the program. Beth told me later, "I know that God honored my faith, but I did something that was really hard." Then she explained the working of God and how it was reflected in her prayers and the prayers of the other kids. "They didn't seem to pray as hard as I prayed, and when God answered, they didn't seem to rejoice as much as I did."

Praying Alone or with Others?

Sometimes we enjoy praying with other people who can really pray. Their voice is strong and they get through when they talk to God.

They strengthen our faith because we know God will hear them, and He will answer. It's good to pray with others because you can experience their faith, and they strengthen your faith to pray stronger.

But it's also good to pray alone. Someone said, "One intercessor alone with God can move any mountain by moving heaven." Didn't Jesus tell us to enter our prayer closet—alone—and to shut the door behind us (see Matt. 6:6)? Jesus promises, "Your Father who sees in secret will reward you openly" (Matt. 6:6).

Which way is the best way to pray? Privately, or with a group? Both are best at different times. You must walk on both your left leg and your right leg to get anywhere. Those who hobble along on one leg don't get very far, nor do they go very fast, nor is their journey enjoyable and efficient.

Left, right . . . left, right . . . left, right . . . left, right . . . it takes both legs to get anywhere. You must learn to pray both with groups and by yourself.

Because prayer is *relationship*, i.e., talking with God, you can talk to God alone or with a group. You can talk to God in the cab of your pick-up, or you can pray inwardly riding the subway in a crowd or waiting in line for a cashier to check out your purchases at a store.

Private prayer reaches God; so learn to pray inwardly by yourself, or pray silently when standing in a crowd. But also learn to agree in prayer with one other person or with many other persons. You can enjoy being lifted on the wings of a prayer with one or when joined with many.

Solo Prayer

As you read this book, you are on a solo journey of faith. No one has joined you and you are symbolically in your private "prayer closet" praying alone, like Beth. Perhaps you are part of a group fast. Many are fasting and praying for a faith project; but even in the middle of a group effort, this is a private journey for you.

Why? Because it's the first time you've fasted, or you have a hard time opening up to pray with others. That's all right! God can hear your solo prayer, because God responds to anyone who prays in sincerity and faith.

I mentioned the prayer closet earlier. *The Living Bible* translates it as "Go away by yourself . . . pray to your Father secretly" (Matt. 6:6). The *Christian Standard Bible* says, "Go into your private room" (Matt. 6:6). Because prayer is an intimate conversation with God, find your personal, usually quiet, place to do it.

Look at the Bible's illustration of Jesus praying: "As He was praying alone" (Luke 9:18), and again, "He departed again to the mountain by Himself alone" (John 6:15). The Gospel of Mark describes this situation: "After saying good-bye to them, he went to the mountain to pray" (Mark 6:46, *NET*).

When you're talking to God, you may be alone, but you're never lonely. The Lord will be there with you to hear you and encourage you.

My Time to Pray

Lord, I come to the private place alone to seek Your presence.
I am fasting and praying for my vow that I've made to You.
Even when others are praying for the same request, my prayer is private
and personal. I bring it to You.
Lord, grant my request I make to You alone. Amen.

My Answers Today

_____
_____
_____
_____
_____
_____
_____
_____
_____

For suggested recipes, see pages 180-192.

❧ DAY 2 ❧

Joining Others in a Daniel Fast

Our ability to perceive God's direction in life is directly related to our ability to sense the inner promptings of His Spirit. God provides a specific activity to assist us in doing this. . . . Men through whom God has worked greatly have emphasized the significance of prayer with fasting. . . . In an extended fast of over three days, one quickly experiences a great decrease in sensual desires and soon has a great new alertness to spiritual things.

BILL GOTHARD

Asking for specific things from God is a rule of His kingdom. Jesus told us, "Ask, and it will be given to you; seek, and you will find; knock, and it will be opened to you" (Matt. 7:7).

Specifically asking is one of the reasons I was converted, and it was motivated by a group of prayer intercessors who prayed throughout most of the summer of 1950. I had just graduated from high school and was accepted into Armstrong Junior College in Savannah, Georgia, with a full scholarship. But prayer was offered for me.

Two twin brothers from Columbia Bible College—Bill and Burt Harding—came to be summer pastors at Bonna Bella Presbyterian Church, about 10 miles from downtown Savannah, and about 5 miles from my home. There was nothing exciting about Bonna Bella, located on a fishing creek with two stores, where streetcar tracks crossed LaRoacha Avenue; but the young twin brothers made Bonna Bella the talk of all Savannah.

I attended a Presbyterian church, and I thought I was saved; I even talked about becoming a minister. But my plans were fluid. I also had won a work scholarship to Georgia Tech University because of some futuristic architectural plans I submitted in a contest.

Little Bonna Bella Presbyterian Church grew from about 20 attendees to more than 50 people under the ministry of Bill and Burt Harding. Groups of teens from different Presbyterian churches around Savannah went to visit the Bonna Bella church because of the excitement going on there.

Bill and Burt Harding lived in a garage apartment over a two-car garage that had a small, screened porch with small wooden stairs leading to the second floor. They held a prayer meeting every morning from 5:00 A.M. to 8:00 A.M. If I had heard about this prayer meeting, I wouldn't have gone. I had never heard of people individually or as a group praying that long.

Bill told the small congregation, "Come and pray on your way to work. You don't need to stay the whole time, nor do you need to come every day."

The brothers convinced the believers in that community that they could change the world by prayer. "You can pray for a young person who'll become a missionary who will take the gospel around the world."

They had a list of about 60 names of young people that they left on the porch to guide the intercessors to pray for each one.

I never went to the prayer meeting, and I only heard about it after I got saved. But that prayer meeting did influence the world.

The brothers would divide the morning prayer shift: one brother would meet prayer warriors from 5:00 A.M. to 6:30 A.M., and the other brother from 6:30 A.M. to 8:00 A.M. The next day they did the reverse.

The porch was small—long and narrow—not more than four or five people could fit on this screened porch, six at the max. There was a big flat grassy yard in front of the garage apartment for parking, which accommodated more cars than people.

The people of Bonna Bella were all blue-collar mill workers, but they were real people. No rich folk there, no millionaires or anyone trying to be a millionaire. They just worked for a paycheck, took care of their families and tried to do right. But they believed Bill and Burt, and they tried to influence the world by praying for revival and for the 60 names on that sheet of paper.

It was still dark at 5:00 A.M. when the first car drove up to the front of the garage apartment and cut off the lights. A solitary figure climbed the stairs in the moonlight and knelt by the springs of an old rusty Army cot. One of the twins knelt by the squeaking old glider, the kind they don't make anymore. He could barely read the names by the yellow insect repellent light bulb in the ceiling. Then he would begin to bang on the windows of heaven:

> Lord, save Elmer Towns . . .
> Lord, save Arthur Winn . . .
> Lord, save L. J. McEwen . . .
> Lord, save Ann Perry . . .
> Lord, save . . .

Then the prayer intercessor would pray for the names on that list, as well as for their little church and for revival, and finally for the world. "Lord, may one of these young persons get saved and influence the world."

In July 1950, the twins invited Joel Ortendahl, their friend from Columbia Bible College, to come preach a week of revival. The first day, Mr. and Mrs. Ernie Miller went forward to get saved. The next night Mrs. Miller stood in the church to give a testimony. "I was a Jehovah's Witness and went all over this neighborhood witnessing for Jehovah. Now I've found Jesus as my Savior, and He is my Jehovah."

"AMEN!" and shouts of "PRAISE THE LORD!" rang over the Presbyterian congregation that was not used to shouting. Then Mrs. Miller continued testifying.

"My husband, Ernest, was born Jewish. He also got saved last night; now he knows Jesus is his Messiah."

"AMEN . . . AMEN!" the shouts lasted twice as long.

That news spread quickly through the teen community. All the young people from our church began visiting the Bonna Bella church: Art Winn, Ann Perry, L. J. McEwen, and me, plus about 20 others from our church.

When Rev. Brian Nicholson wrote a doctoral project from Reformed Theological Seminary, he noted that 19 young people from Eastern Heights Presbyterian Church went into full-time ministry.[1] These 19 were saved at the Bonna Bella revival. That only represented one congregation of young people on that list of 60 for which the Harding brothers and their group of early morning intercessors prayed.

About the third or fourth night of the revival, a middle-aged man went forward for salvation. After the service, all the new converts stood in front of the church and were introduced to the audience. He said, "You don't need to introduce me, you all know me; I'm your mailman." He told of driving down LaRoacha Avenue toward the church when he felt heat coming from the Presbyterian church building. As he drove past the building, the heat went away. This happened every day the revival was going on.

Later in life, I understood this to be the *atmospheric presence* of God. You can walk into a church where God is working and feel His presence, just as you can feel wet atmosphere outside on an overcast day when it's not raining.

The mailman said he had to come to the revival meeting to find out what was going on. He testified, "I was baptized in a Baptist church as a teenager and since have become a Baptist Sunday School teacher and a Baptist deacon; but tonight I got born again . . . Hallelujah, I'm saved!" More Presbyterian shouts of "AMEN!" and "HALLELUJAH!"

On July 25, 1950, I received Christ as Savior. I refused to go forward, thinking I was saved. But under tremendous conviction of sin, I had to do something. No one went forward that Thursday night. Bill Harding walked to the Communion table and said, "Someone is supposed to come forward tonight and give your heart to Christ, but you say no!'"

I knew Bill was talking to me. He said, "Go home, kneel by your bed, look up into heaven and say, 'Jesus, come into my heart and save me.'"

I made that prayer about 11:15 that evening and I knew instantly that I was born again. My life has never been the same.

You can pray just like those people gathered in the garage apartment screened porch. You can change the world through your Daniel Prayer. Maybe you've taken a vow to fast for a particular answer to prayer, or you've joined with others to trust God for a particular goal.

God loves unity, that's why Jesus told His disciples, "Tarry in the city of Jerusalem until you are endued with power" (Luke 24:49). What did they do? "These all continued with one accord in prayer" (Acts 1:14). They followed the instruction of the Lord, and the Holy Spirit filled each one on the day of Pentecost (see Acts 2:1-4).

Notice how the church in the book of Acts came together in prayer: "When they had prayed, the place where they were assembled together was shaken" (Acts 4:31). Again, "But while Peter was kept in the prison, the church prayed very earnestly for him" (Acts 12:5, *NLT*).

The same results can happen when you separately pledge yourself to a prayer goal and when you unite with others in unity to see God work in your midst. When many agree on a Daniel Fast, God honors their faith. "If two [or more] of you agree on earth concerning anything that they ask, it will be done for them by My Father in heaven" (Matt. 18:19).

My Time to Pray

Lord, I join myself to others to fast and intercede for a prayer goal;
give me the request I ask.

May I strengthen the faith of others as they reciprocate to strengthen my
faith; together we fast and intercede for our prayer goal.

Lord, I come privately to You, even when I am in the prayer company
of others, to ask for the prayer goal for which I vowed. Amen.

My Answers Today

_____
_____
_____
_____
_____
_____
_____
_____
_____
_____
_____
_____
_____
_____
_____
_____
_____
_____

Note

1. Brian Nicholson, "History of Providence Presbyterian Church, Savannah Georgia," a theology project for Reformed Theological Seminary, Jackson, Mississippi.

For suggested recipes, see pages 180-192.

❧ DAY 3 ❧

Daily Commitment During Your Fast

*Fasting can strengthen your faith and draw you closer to God,
helping you to be a true overcomer in Christ. Fasting is a true gift to
Christians who desire to be more effective in prayer.*

ELMER TOWNS

The decision you make to God as you enter the Daniel Fast is much more important than what food you choose to stop eating or what other activity you sacrifice to God.

The original fast by Daniel is described in *The New Living Translation* as follows: "Daniel made up his mind not to defile himself by eating the food and wine given to them by the king" (Dan. 1:8). The *New International Version* says, "Daniel resolved," while the *New King James Version* says, "Daniel purposed," and the *CSB* says, "Daniel determined." All of these synonyms point to a life-changing decision of the will. Your Daniel Fast will be effective when you make a life-changing commitment—throughout this book I call it a vow—that you will modify your food or activities while you intercede for your prayer goal.

You have made an original vow to fast and pray for a faith project. Now you must make a daily choice to continue your fast.

Remember, a choice involves all of your personality: your intellect, emotions and will. You first know with your mind, but knowledge by itself is not enough to change your life, nor will it get the prayer goal you seek. Your emotions can be stirred for this fast, but getting excited may only change the surface things. You may change a few things—while you're excited—but what about the long haul? Your life will be transformed when your will makes a choice based on what your mind knows, and when your emotions are stirred toward the prayer goal.

You don't have the power to obey
until you make a choice to obey.

I learned the power of choice from my junior Sunday School teacher growing up in Eastern Heights Presbyterian Church of Savannah, Georgia. My teacher, Jimmy Breland, saturated our minds with the Bible. We memorized and repeated a Bible verse every Sunday, plus I memorized the Westminster Children's Catechism (a summary of basic theology). It seemed I learned every list in the Bible: the 12 disciples, the 12 tribes of Israel, the days of creation, the plagues on the Egyptians, the 22 kings of Judah, and so on. But knowing the Bible didn't change my life.

Next, Jimmy Breland told stories to stir our emotions—stories to make us laugh, cry and some that scared me about sin and hell. But stirring my emotions didn't change my life.

After telling a story of how Jacob disobeyed his parents, Jimmy said to us, "Raise your right hand and repeat after me . . ." I did as he requested, and repeated the following:

I promise . . .
to always obey my mother,
so help me, God.

As I lowered my hand, I asked myself, *What have I just said?* I struggled with obedience, as do most small boys. I examined my heart, asking, *Will I always obey my mother no matter what?*

On successive Sundays in Jimmy Breland's class, I raised my right hand and promised not to shoplift, not to lie, not to smoke, not to drink beer, and so on.

Jimmy Breland was the most influential teacher I ever had because he filled my mind with Scripture, stirred my emotions with stories and made me pledge to do right by raising my right hand with a promise to God.

When I was about 10 years old, I went to hang out in a corner store about a block from my house. My hand brushed across a box of Milky Ways on a low counter. The thought crossed my mind, *I could have stolen that candy car, and the lady behind the counter would have never seen me do it.*

That night I lay in my bed and thought about stealing a Milky Way. It was extremely tempting if you were as poor as my family was. We almost never had money for candy bars.

The next day I made a trial run. I picked up a Milky Way when the lady clerk wasn't looking. I held that chocolate nougat prize in my hand almost like a drunk fingering a glass of whisky. I put it back and walked out the store without stealing, thinking, *I can do this.*

The following Sunday, Jimmy Breland taught a lesson on stealing and casually said, "I don't want any of you stealing a Milky Way from a store."

Who told him . . . ? I immediately panicked. I felt as caught as if I had completed the crime.

Then it came to me, *I didn't tell anyone.* So I asked myself, *How did he know?* The realization came to me.

God told him.

Even in my 10-year-old mind, I had a God-consciousness that brought great guilt. I realized God knew the thoughts of our hearts. So Jimmy Breland made us lift our hands and say:

I promise . . .
I will never steal . . .
From a store . . .
So help me, God.

Unknown to Jimmy Breland or the other members of the class, I added, *I will never steal a Milky Way.* I purposed in my heart, just as Daniel purposed in his heart.

There are five things you need to commit to God in this fast. If you haven't done it yet, you should give to God the following five things: time, temple, talent, testimony and treasure.

First, you should commit your fast *time* to God. Pledge to begin and end according to the time limit you set in the checklist. If you are following the Daniel Fast with a group, promise to stay on your fast as long as the group fasts. *Lord, I promise to withhold food or other activities as long as my fast lasts.*

The second aspect of your Daniel Fast is your *temple.* You have pledged to eat healthy during this fast. You must commit your bodily temple to God. *Lord, I give my physical body to You. I will not eat or drink anything that will harm my body. I will refrain from alcohol, drugs, addiction and gluttony.*

The third part of your life to commit to God is your *talent,* or your abilities. In the Daniel Fast, this is committing your prayer ability to God. You must go beyond everything you have known about God and prayer in the past. You must pray many ways[1] and at many times. *Lord, I promise to keep my prayer time during this fast. Help me learn to pray more effectively, and help me learn the intimacy of Your presence.*

The fourth aspect of your commitment is your *testimony.* Those who have joined you in your prayer goal will be watching you. You can be an encouragement to them as they are an encouragement to you. Be strong for all your friends who are watching you. *Lord, fill my life with Your presence. Help me keep my fast strong to the end. Use my fast as a testimony to encourage others. May others see Christ in me.*

The fifth area is your *treasure,* or your money. Obviously, you are giving tithes and offerings to God, and usually through your church. If you're not, remember the challenge of God, " 'Bring all the tithes into the storehouse . . . and try Me now in this,' says the LORD of hosts, 'If I will not open for you the windows of heaven And pour out for you *such* blessing' " (Mal. 3:10). Remember, when you give all your money to God, He lets you use 90 percent for your needs. The 10 percent is used for His work. *Lord, I give all my treasures to You. Use them in Your work.*

As you continue your Daniel Fast, you will face many temptations to quit. Remember, quitting is a decision just as beginning was a decision. However, the greatness of your decision to begin will outweigh any temptation to decide to quit. There's a lot to lose by quitting, and there is everything to gain by continuing to the end. You'll never know the completeness of what God will do if you give up too soon. You'll never know the joy of a job well done if you are not firm to the end.

My Time to Pray

Lord, I have purposed in my heart to intercede for a prayer goal;
I will not give up.

Lord, I will not give in to my appetite to break my Daniel Fast.
I will be strong to the end.

Lord, I need Your strength to empower me. Help me realize, "I can do all
things through Christ who strengthens me" (Phil. 4:13). Amen.

My Answers Today

_____

_____

_____

_____

_____

_____

_____

_____

_____

Note

1. To learn many ways to pray, read *How to Pray When You Don't Know What to Say* by Elmer Towns, Regal Books, Ventura, California, 2006. To order the book, contact Regal Books (www.regalbooks.com) or phone 1-800-4-GOSPEL.

For suggested recipes, see pages 180-192.

❧ DAY 4 ❧

Praying and Fasting for a Project

Fasting has gone almost completely out of the life of the ordinary person.
Jesus condemned the wrong kind of fasting, but He never meant that fasting
should be completely eliminated from life and living. We would do well to
practice it in our own way and according to our own need.
WILLIAM BARCLAY

Have you joined the Daniel Fast because you are praying for a proj-ect? If so, you need to know that you are not the first to fast and pray for a project. Many others have done the same thing. We will look at Ezra because he fasted and prayed to solve a particular problem facing him. We will learn some helpful principles from him to make fasting more effective.

As I write this chapter, I am fasting and asking God to lead me. I did not eat dinner last night, nor am I eating breakfast or lunch today. I'm spending my meal times in prayer for this project.

The book of Ezra tells how the Jews returned to the Promised Land after 70 years of captivity. God had used Nebuchadnezzar, king of Babylon, to punish God's people, primarily because of their idolatry, but other sins also sent them into captivity. Neb-uchadnezzar destroyed Jerusalem and sent the majority of Jews to Babylon.

Almost 100 years later, the nations of Media-Persia defeated Babylon, and their King Cyrus of Persia gave a decree for Jews to return to their homeland and rebuild their Temple. Zerubbabel led the first wave of refugees back and began work on the Temple. The surrounding nations caused trouble, and the rebuilding went slowly but was finished in 515 B.C.

Then Ezra, a priest, attempted to lead a group back, and he gathered some Levites to accompany him. They gathered on the banks of the Ahava River (see Ezra 8:15) near the Euphrates River. To return to Israel, they had to cross the unrelenting desert and leave civilization along the mighty Euphrates.

Ezra faced a problem that seemed insurmountable. The desert was inhabited with savage nomadic tribes; many were gangs of thieves who attacked caravans for their treasure. Ezra confessed, "I was ashamed to ask the king to send soldiers and cavalry to protect us against enemies along the way" (Ezra 8:22, CEV).

This was similar to wagon trains of American settlers that needed the protection of the U.S. Cavalry when they crossed Indian Territory in the nineteenth century. But Ezra had compounded the problem by boasting, "After all, we had told the king that our God takes care of everyone who truly worships him" (Ezra 8:22, CEV). This set up their need to fast for safety.

Ezra had approximately 4,000 people he was leading back home. These Jews had gone to their relatives and friends who were not returning to receive an offering of money or valuables to rebuild the Temple. It was a huge offering: "In all there were: 25 tons of silver; 100 silver articles weighing 150 pounds; 7,500 pounds of gold; 20 gold bowls weighing 270 ounces; and 2 polished bronze articles as valuable as gold" (Ezra 8:26, CEV).

What would you do if faced with this threatening problem? "So we went without food and asked God Himself to protect us" (Ezra 8:23, CEV). This was not an individual problem, but involved a large scope of national significance. Also, the house of God was at stake. Remember, a private problem involves a private fast; a family problem involves a family fast; and a national problem involves a national fast.

How large is the Daniel Fast for which you are praying? Is the progress of God's work at stake? Is personal spiritual growth at stake? Is there danger of loss if the fast is not successful? Is God's honor at stake?

Principles for Fasting for a Project

Step 1: Find those who will fast for the project. Most likely, you are already in a Daniel Fast and you are already committed to the project. So the first thing is to find those who are also burdened for the project. You should fast and pray with others.

Step 2: Share the problem. If people are going to fast for a problem, they must either know about it or be involved in the project. Ezra said, "I proclaimed a fast . . . that we might humble ourselves before our God, to seek from Him the right way for us and our little ones and all our possessions" (Ezra 8:21). They fasted because they had a legitimate reason to be scared. The greater the number of people who feel the problem, the more likely they will be to fast for the project.

Step 3: Fast seriously. Ezra communicated the seriousness of the problem to the people. So when they understood their danger, they willingly fasted and prayed for protection. Ezra challenged them, "that we might afflict ourselves before our God" (Ezra 8:21, *KJV*). The word "afflicted" in this verse contains the idea of sorrow, mourning and repentance. When Israel fasted, they usually faced a life-threatening danger or a drought or pestilence. It was then the people fasted seriously. Then fasting was not a burden but their only means of deliverance.

FASTING PRODUCES
Spiritual introspection
Spiritual examination
Spiritual confession
Spiritual intercession

Step 4: Fast before attempting a solution. Often we wait until we get into a problem, then we try to get out of it any way possible. We borrow money, ask a friend to help, work overtime or cut back on expenses. After these don't work, we pray about the problem.

Finally, when prayer doesn't seem to be working, we fast, taking prayer to its higher level.

Fasting shouldn't be the last thing we try in desperation. No! We ought to fast about a problem before it becomes a problem. We need to try *defensive fasting*. Ezra did something before even trying to solve the problem: "I gathered them by the river that flows to Ahava, and we camped there three days" (Ezra 8:15). Notice what he didn't do:

> He did not fast as he traveled.
> He did not fast alone before gathering the people.
> He did not try to solve the problem before fasting.

This suggests that you must recognize the spiritual nature of your problem before you begin to solve it. Actually, we ought to develop a "fasting mentality," which means we develop an attitude of dependence on God for all the times we do not fast.

Step 5: Fast on-site with insight. A new movement called "prayer walking" has developed in modern Christianity. This is praying on-site with insight. This means you will pray more seriously when you actually see your problem with your eyes than when you think about it or even when you try to see it in your mind.

When you stand in a place of need,
you will pray with more heed.

Actually, prayer walking was practiced in Scripture. God told Abraham to walk through the land that He—the LORD God—was going to give him (see Gen. 13:17). Also, God instructed Joshua to walk around the city of Jericho once each day for seven days, then seven times on the seventh day. Also, Joshua was told to walk throughout the land that he was going to conquer (see Josh. 1:3-9).

Ezra brought the people face to face with their problems, that is, to the banks of the Ahava River, before they launched out into the desert. Perhaps after staring at the desert for three days, the people were more challenged to fast and pray. "Beside the Ahava

River, I asked the people to go without eating and to pray" (Ezra 8:21, *CEV*).

Step 6: Fast and pray for a step-by-step guidance. They fasted before entering the problem where they could think and plan more intelligently. In the midst of a problem we usually don't think accurately or predicatively.

If you can break down a large problem into smaller issues, you usually can solve the smaller problems easier and faster than the larger problem. So do that before a problem surrounds you or you're drowning in a sea of red ink.

Before the problem hits you, pray not only for a final solution to the whole problem but also for God's guidance through the step-by-step solutions to the smaller problems along the way. There were many routes Ezra could have taken to Jerusalem, just as there is usually more than one way to solve your problem. Probably some roads were more traveled than others; some roads were more frequently traveled by soldiers or fierce tribes that could help fight back against thieves. As a result, some roads were safer than others.

Ezra called a fast, "to seek from Him the right way for us" (Ezra 8:21). The Bible teaches that God's sovereignty guides our ways, but we should use common sense along the way. "We draw our maps to the destination, but God directs each step along the road" (Prov. 16:9, *ELT*).

So why did Ezra and his entourage fast? "We went without food and asked God himself to protect us" (Ezra 8:23, *CEV*).

Step 7: Use common sense. Ezra had a tremendous amount of money to deliver to Jerusalem. It was not his money, nor did it belong to the travelers with him. It was God's money. So Ezra used his ingenuity. He divided up the money among the travelers so that everyone carried some of the money. If they were attacked, he reasoned, at least those who got through safely could deliver God's money to Jerusalem. "[I] weighed out to them the silver, the gold, and the articles, the offering for the house of our God which the king and his counselors and his princes, and all Israel who were present, had offered. I weighed into their hand six hundred and fifty talents of silver, silver articles weighing one hundred talents, one hundred talents of gold, twenty gold basins worth a thousand drachmas, and two vessels of fine polished bronze, precious as gold" (Ezra 8:25-27).

Ezra charged those with God's money, "You are holy to the LORD; the articles are holy also" (Ezra 8:28). He reminded them the money belonged to God, and so did they.

Ezra's common sense applied to the accountability of each one who was carrying God's money. It's so easy for those handling God's money to use it wrongly or use it for their own purpose, or even let a little stick to sticky fingers. (The stickiness is found in the heart, not on the fingers.) When they arrived in Jerusalem, they counted the money, "A receipt was given for each item, and the weight of the gold and silver was noted" (Ezra 8:34, *TLB*).

Just because Ezra was a spiritual man doesn't mean he was naïve. A cash register causes employees to be honest. Two or more counting the church offering makes people accountable to the other persons and ultimately accountable to God. What happened to Ezra and the people? "So we fasted and entreated our God for this, and He answered our prayer" (Ezra 8:23).

My Time to Pray

Lord, I will fast for big projects before I attempt to solve them.

Lord, I will examine all facts and try to understand a problem, then I'll ask You to give me insight how to solve my problems.

Lord, I will seek to break big problems down into smaller ones, then work on them one at a time. Help me use my common sense to solve my problems.

Lord, I will love all people; but when it comes to money, I'll make them accountable because I want them to be honest.

Lord, I will fast, and I will rejoice in Your goodness after You have honored my fast and answered my prayer. Amen.

My Answers Today

_____

_____

_____

_____

_____

_____

_____

_____

_____

_____

_____

_____

_____

_____

_____

_____

For suggested recipes, see pages 180-192.

❖ DAY 5 ❖

The Benefits of a Lengthy Fast

*In those days I, Daniel, was mourning three full weeks. I didn't eat
any rich food, no meat or wine entered my mouth, and I didn't put
any oil on my body until the three weeks were over.*

DANIEL 10:2-3, *CSB*

How long should you fast? Some people fast for one day; some
fast for 10 days; others fast for 21 days; a few fast for 40 days.

I fast on a regular basis, following the Old Testament sequence
of fasting, i.e., from sundown to sundown. This is called the Yom
Kippur fast, for all Jews were commanded to fast on that day. "On
the tenth day of the seventh month of each year, you must go without eating to show sorrow for your sins" (Lev. 16:29, *CEV*). The Jews
got their lead from God Himself who said the days of creation began, "The evening and the morning were the first day" (Gen. 1:5).

Usually, the more pressing a problem, the longer I fast. When
I have a serious need, I fast longer than one day. My one-day fast
is just to know God more intimately.

The Daniel Fast is usually 10 or 21 days. On both occasions
he faced a great challenge, so he answered with a great commitment to prayer.

For the first fast, Daniel challenged the Babylonian official
over him, "Please test your servants . . . ten days, and let them give
us vegetables to eat and water to drink" (Dan. 1:12).

Later in life (probably in his nineties) Daniel described a 21-day fast: "I, Daniel, was mourning three full weeks. I ate no pleasant food, no meat or wine came into my mouth, nor did I anoint myself at all, till three whole weeks were fulfilled" (Dan. 10:2-3).

It seems that the first time Daniel fasted for 10 days, it was a time preset by him. The second fast seems to reflect a period of time given to prayer, mourning and seeking God for an answer. An angel was sent to Daniel on the twenty-first day, saying, "Do not fear, Daniel, for from the first day that you set your heart to understand, and to humble yourself before your God, your words were heard; and I have come because of your words" (Dan. 10:12).

Probably you are fasting with a group from your church or, perhaps, another organization. Someone else has set the time for this Daniel Fast, either 10 or 21 days. (God will not measure the success of your fast just because you fast for 10 or 21 days. God looks at the quality time you spend in His presence and then rewards you by the biblical nature of your intercession.)

For whatever the length of your Daniel Fast, join in willingly and submit to your spiritual leadership (see Heb. 13:17). Never complain about the length, or about any other aspect of what your group is practicing in this fast. *Lord, I will fast strong to the end.*

The Benefits of a Lengthy Fast

First of all, ask how serious is the fasting goal for which you are praying. If it is an extremely imperative goal, then obviously you want to spend as much time in prayer as possible to make sure God hears and God answers. Sometimes God doesn't respond to a quickly breathed prayer when we squeeze Him into our otherwise busy schedule.

Yes, God heard the desperate prayer of Peter who began to sink beneath the storm's waves. His prayer for help was filled with panic because the situation was life threatening. Obviously, a quickly breathed prayer is effective, but we probably need to pray longer over hard-to-solve problems. Why? Because it takes a longer time to solve some problems. So ask yourself, *How serious is this prayer goal?* If it's serious and imperative, then commit yourself to a 10- or 21-day time limit, and determine to stay with it to the end.

Second, your prayer will grow in intensity as the fast time unrolls. You'll develop more faith with time. Fasting for 10 or 21 days is like running a race; the closer to the finish line, the more your adrenaline begins to flow and you give it a "kick" to finish the race.

As you pray through your Daniel Fast, you'll probably keep up with the prayers toward the beginning. Usually, we lag in the middle of a fast. But toward the end, our prayer intensity kicks in. Maybe it's because money is being raised, or a sick person begins to recover, or progress is made toward completion of a goal. With any success, you will be motivated to pray deeper or to pray with more urgency toward the end of your fast.

Sometimes there is little or no progress toward the faith goal. This is the time some get discouraged and quit. If nothing is happening, some people dial down their prayer intensity. Human nature being what it is, some need outward stimulation to keep praying or even to continue their Daniel Fast to the end.

But remember, you didn't vow a pledge to a group or to a church. Your faith pledge for the Daniel Fast was made to God. Don't you think God knew the success of the project before you made your pledge or before the goal was set? Then fast to the end of your pledge to please God.

Then there's another factor: Be true to yourself. If you've pledged for 10 or 21 days, then you owe it to your integrity to keep your word. If you quit too soon, your self-perception is blurred and your self-determination is weakened. You might not keep your word on another promise completely unrelated to fasting.

There's a third reason you need time to fast: It takes time for your faith to grow. The more you pray about a project, the sharper your faith will become.

Look at Abraham! When God first called him and promised to build a nation through his children, the Bible describes him as "weak in faith" (Rom. 4:19). Didn't he go to Egypt and allow his wife to be taken into Pharaoh's harem? Didn't he compromise with Hagar, an Egyptian concubine?

But God patiently strengthened Abraham's faith so that he believed God could do what God promised. "And not being weak in faith . . . he did not waver at the promise of God through unbelief, but was strengthened in faith, giving glory to God" (Rom. 4:19-20).

Perhaps you have weak faith as you begin your Daniel Fast. But as you continue fasting—day after day—you'll find your faith being strengthened as you learn how to pray.

At another place, Paul reminds us our faith should be moving from one kind of faith to a stronger kind of faith. Paul tells us, "From faith to faith; as it is written, 'The just shall live by faith'" (Rom. 1:17).

So why fast for 10 days, or even for 21 days? You probably will begin your fast with immature faith. Maybe all you know for sure is that Jesus has saved you, God is your Father and the Holy Spirit guides you. But you can grow to intercession-faith so that you can get through to God as you fast and pray. You can grow "from faith to faith" in this Daniel Fast. It may take the total of 21 days until you have strong enough faith to pray boldly.

If your faith is weak faith (see Rom. 14:1), then begin praying daily, as the father who didn't have enough faith to heal his son but wanted his son healed. He prayed, "Lord, I believe; help thou mine unbelief" (Mark 9:24, *KJV*).

A fourth reason to fast a long time is so the project can grow in your mind. If someone else has set your fast goal, maybe you're not as burdened as the leader of your group, or your pastor. Maybe you are fasting for a new sanctuary at church or an evangelistic project, or some other goal. When other people set a goal, it's not felt as deeply as if you set it yourself—especially if it's for your personal ministry.

So a lengthy time of fasting and prayer will focus the goal in your heart. You will probably feel a growing burden as you continue to fast for your goal. It may take time for God to speak to your heart and show you the importance of the goal.

The longer you pray for the fast goal, the clearer you will see how God will use the goal to expand His kingdom and glorify Himself.

Keep your physical eyes open as you look at the documents of your goal. If you can, go to the place—walk around the area for which you are praying. I call this geographical praying. God may use circumstances at the place of your faith goal to intensify your prayer urgency for the goal.

There's another thing that geographical praying does for you. It revives your recessive memory. Many memories will be revived when you pray at the place for which you are praying. You may have been saved at that prayer altar, or God may have redirected your life at that location.

The fifth benefit of a lengthy fast is that it usually takes time to find sin in your life and deal with it by the blood of Christ. There may be a sin hidden in your heart, or you may be blinded to an otherwise obvious sin. Remember, "If I regard iniquity in my heart, The Lord will not hear" (Ps. 66:18). Because we justify some of our sin, we don't see the hidden sin in our heart that hinders answers to prayer.

As you tarry in God's presence, realize, "God does not hear sinners" (John 9:31) and "Your iniquities have separated you from your God; And your sins have hidden His face from you, So that He will not hear" (Isa. 59:2).

Remember, you have an enemy who opposes you. Satan doesn't want you to be holy and separated from sin. He doesn't want you to get answers to prayers. He doesn't want you to enjoy intimacy with God. Satan blinds you to sin in your life so that you will not repent of sin. He uses satanic blindness to keep you in his grasp: "The god of this age has blinded, [those] who do not believe, lest the light of the gospel of the glory of Christ, who is the image of God, should shine on them" (2 Cor. 4:4).

So, you need to pray with David, "Search me, O God . . . And see if there is any wicked way in me" (Ps. 139:23-24). It may take time for God to reveal to you the one hidden sin that blocks His blessing in your life.

You can be sure that if you ask God to show you your sin, He will do it: "There is nothing covered that will not be revealed, and hidden that will not be known" (Matt. 10:26). Therefore, don't be impatient if God doesn't answer your prayer (accompanied with fasting) the first time you pray, or even the first day of your fast. It may take 10 days, or even 21 days.

Finally, the sixth reason why you have a lengthy fast is that it takes time to search for God and find Him. When you search for something, it's because you've lost it and you need it. Searching suggests a deep desire on our part.

At times, God doesn't immediately disclose Himself. The psalmist exclaims, "Why do You hide Your face?" (Ps. 44:24). Perhaps God hides to see if we really want to find Him.

My Time to Pray

Lord, open my spiritual eyes progressively throughout this fast so that I may know You better at the end than I did at the beginning.

Lord, as I wait in Your presence, reveal to me any sin lurking in my heart that would hinder my prayers.

Lord, give me a resolute heart to pray continually, to pray sincerely and to pray in faith.

Lord, I vow not to give up until the end of this fast. Amen.

My Answers Today

_____
_____
_____
_____
_____
_____
_____
_____
_____

For suggested recipes, see pages 180-192.

❦ DAY 6 ❦

Saying No in Prayer

*Fasting is the most powerful spiritual discipline of all the Christian disciplines.
Through fasting and prayer, the Holy Spirit can transform your life.
Fasting and prayer can also work on a much grander scale. According to
Scripture, personal experience and observation, I am convinced that when God's
people fast with a proper biblical motive—seeking God's face not His hand—
with a broken, repentant and contrite spirit, God will hear from heaven and
heal our lives, our churches, our communities, our nation and world. Fasting and
prayer can bring about revival—a change in the direction of our nation,
the nations of earth and the fulfillment of the Great Commission.*

BILL BRIGHT

The word "afflict" is tied to fasting on several occasions. The first time a believer is told to fast is in Leviticus 16:29. The old *King James* says, "Ye shall afflict your souls." *The Living Bible* says, "Spend the day in self-examination and humility." The *Holman Christian Standard Bible* translates it, "You are to practice self-denial." The word "afflict" is constantly tied to fasting (see Lev. 16:29,34; Num. 29:7; Isa. 58:3,5).

The word "afflict" in the dictionary means "to cause distress, to cause anguish or suffering."[1] Therefore, when you give up something pleasurable, you bring some discomfort or distress upon yourself.

Why do we do this? It's not that we love pain. We do it for a spiritual reason. We do it to pray more earnestly for a faith project.

When we afflict ourselves, it's none of the masochistic things some extremists have done. It's not whipping ourselves with whips, or punishing the flesh to keep it submitted to God.

When we afflict ourselves, we say no to the sinful flesh. This is another way to express repentance. To afflict yourself expresses the desire to rid your life of sinful things. It's a way of dealing with sinful attitudes.

Why "afflict"? Sometimes we love doing sin more than serving God. We love thinking about our sin more than meditating on God. So we must repent of our actions. After all, the word "repentance" means "to turn from."

So when we fast, pray and afflict ourselves, we say no to our previous sins, and we say yes to God and His will for our lives.

Sometimes we are blind to our sin. A wrong attitude creeps into our thought life, and we don't immediately recognize it as sin. That's the way termites get into a house—unnoticed.

A neighbor of mine, about 15 years ago, discovered that some snakes had crawled inside the walls of his house into the attic. He killed one or two with traps but discovered more. So he had to deal severely with the problem. He moved out for almost a week, had a large tent placed over the house and gassed the snakes (and every other insect). It took severe action to deal with a severe problem.

Hidden sin secretly slips into our life. Sin destroys our walk with God and eats away our Christian character. So when we "afflict" ourselves by fasting, we give God an opportunity to expose sin for what it really is.

We also afflict ourselves of good things. You have made a vow to give up certain things for the Daniel Fast. Maybe you've given up one or two meals a day. Maybe you're eating just vegetables, or you've given up some other practices. The things you've given up are probably all good things. You haven't given them up because they are sinful; and probably these good things don't have a sinful hold on your life.

So, why do we give up good things? We "afflict" ourselves so that we can put God first in our life. We say no to good things so that we can say yes to the best things.

Technically, the Hebrew word for fast is *tsom*, which means to lose one's appetite for food. Suppose you got an emergency phone call that your spouse was in the emergency room at the hospital.

As you begin to rush there, you realize it is past your lunchtime. Would you drive through the pick-up window to grab a hamburger and cold drink? No! The emergency would overwhelm your appetite and you wouldn't even think of eating. That's the true meaning of afflicting yourself for a spiritual burden. You don't even think about eating. In this passage the word "afflict" is translated "weeping and mourning."

Fasting is also identified in Scripture with a solemn assembly. When hurting people come together in a meeting called "a solemn assembly," this is not a time to praise God or worship Him. Nor is it a time to sing psalms of the greatness of God, nor to be instructed in God's Word. A solemn assembly is a time to search the heart for hidden sin and to confess sins and repent of them. These types of meetings go on for hours with people begging God to forgive and restore them to His favor. The book of Joel explains the seriousness of a solemn assembly: "Now, therefore," says the LORD, "Turn to Me with all your heart, With fasting, with weeping, and with mourning . . . So rend your heart, and not your garments" (Joel 2:12-13).

Before we can establish any credible basis for God answering our prayers, we must establish inward character. We do that by examining our hearts as we fast before God.

Also, we must deal with our pride. When we fast for the glory of God, we can say no to our selfish desire to be number one. Jesus said, "But seek first the kingdom of God and His righteousness, and all these things shall be added to you" (Matt. 6:33). So the good things He gives us may be the things we give up for only a season.

When you take control of your outward body by fasting,
you begin to take control of your inward person.

There are two things that should happen when you say no. The negative repentance is what you abstain. You turn from sin. Christ gives you the power to say no whether you say no to a sinful thing or whether you say no to something as good as one or two meals a day. But there is a positive action. Remember, "I can do all things through Christ who strengthens me" (Phil. 4:13).

Christ is in your heart because of salvation. So you yield to His inward strength and let Him give you strength to complete your Daniel Fast. "Thanks be to God who always leads us in triumph in Christ" (2 Cor. 2:14). When you say no to some good things, it's a reminder who's the boss in your life. Sometimes we go through life thinking, *I've got to eat three square meals a day,* or *I deserve that entertainment* or *Everyone else is doing it; why can't I?* While these are good things, and there's nothing wrong with them, the issue is, who's running your life? This is another way of asking, Who's sitting on the throne of your heart? Make sure that:

> *When you give up some good things in life,*
> *you replace them with God who is best for your life.*

My Time to Pray

Lord, I will give up good things to seek Your best in my life.

Lord, as I fast, show me any sinful attitude or action that's hiding in my life. I will say no to it and repent of it.

Lord, the good things I give up cannot be compared with the wonderful privilege of enjoying Your presence. Amen.

My Answers Today

_____

_____

_____

_____

_____

_____

Note
 1. See http://www.merriam-webster.com/dictionary/AFFLICT, s.v. "afflict" (accessed July 17, 2009).

For suggested recipes, see pages 180-192.

DAY 7

The Persistence of a Daniel Fast

There are those who think that fasting belongs to the old dispensation;
but when we look at Acts 14:23 and Acts 13:2-3, we find that it was practiced
by the earnest men of the apostolic day. If we would pray with power, we
should pray with fasting. This, of course, does not mean that we should fast
every time we pray; but there are times of emergency or special crisis in work
or in our individual lives, when men of downright earnestness will withdraw
themselves even from the gratification of natural appetites that would be
perfectly proper under other circumstances, that they may give themselves
wholly to prayer. There is a peculiar power in such prayer. Every great crisis
in life and work should be met that way. There is nothing pleasing to God in
our giving up in a purely Pharisaic and legal way things which are pleasant,
but there is power in that downright earnestness and determination to obtain
in prayer the things of which we sorely feel our need, that leads us to put away
everything, even things in themselves most right and necessary, that we may
set our faces to find God, and obtain blessings from Him.

R. A. TORREY

There are so many distractions in modern life to keep us from praying. Sometimes it's just good things that make us stop praying. There seems to be a television set always telling us of a news disaster or selling us something or demanding our attention. Everywhere we go the cell phone interrupts us or we hear a loudspeaker in the background interrupting our thoughts. When do we ever get a little time to meditate on God? How can we listen to God when there are so many voices competing for our attention? How can we keep on praying when it seems as if everything is competing for our mind?

When you fast, you "come apart" from the bustle of life to commune with God. You seek quietness during the three meal times each day to first listen to God's Word and to His inner voice. Your fast project is a perfect time to seek God for the prayer project you seek.

Jesus tells the story of a man sleeping when his neighbor knocked frantically at his door to borrow some bread in the middle of the night. He replied, "Leave me alone, I'm sleeping and so is my family."

The neighbor kept pounding until he got the bread he sought. Jesus concluded, "Though he will not rise and give to him because he is his friend, yet because of his persistence he will rise and give him as many as he needs. So I say to you, ask, and it will be given to you; seek, and you will find; knock, and it will be opened to you" (Luke 11:8-9).

Many years ago, I learned this verse by remembering the first letters of Ask, Seek and Knock in the acronym ASK, which is another biblical term for praying.

Notice that Jesus commanded us to ask, seek, knock. All three involve persistence expressed in different ways. To ask is to use words to get what you want. To seek is to use your feet to go to where the prize is located. To knock is the idea of using all your body and mind to locate what has been hidden from you.

Think of why we parents hide things from our children. We hide Easter eggs so they will have the thrill of discovery. Maybe that's why God wants you to fast and pray for 10 or 21 days.

Parents hide Christmas gifts till the right moment because they know the kids will appreciate the gift that is appropriately given. So you may have to pray for the entire 21 days to receive and appreciate your faith project.

God may want you to pray for a project for 10 days or even 21 days. Why? The Lord honors persistent prayer. Regardless of fatigue, obstacles, discouragement or doubt, keep praying. When you enter God's presence with an iron will, determine to pray to the end. God will honor your determination and faith.

Wesley L. Duwel, in his book *Prevailing Prayer*, gives us insight into the heart of persistent prayer:

> To prevail is to be successful in the face of difficulty, to completely dominate, to overcome and tie up. Prevailing prayer is prayer that pushes right through all difficulties and obstacles and drives back all the opposing forces of Satan, and secures the will of God. Its purpose is to accomplish God's will on earth. Prevailing prayer not only takes the initiative, but continues on the offence for God until spiritual victory is won.[1]

Why must we prevail? Because God knows the flesh is weak and it's human to give up. The night before Jesus died, He took His disciples into the garden of Gethsemane to pray. He told them to "watch with Me" (Matt. 26:38). What did He say when He found them asleep?

> Then He came to the disciples and found them sleeping, and said to Peter, "What! Could you not watch with Me one hour? Watch and pray, lest you enter into temptation. The spirit indeed is willing, but the flesh is weak" (Matt. 26:40-41).

Jesus knows that your physical body is not trained to keep a 10- or 21-day fast. He will help you do it if you pray and ask Him to strengthen you: "I can do all things through Christ who strengthens me" (Phil. 4:13). So begin this fast with a commitment to complete it.

God may not immediately answer your prayer, because if He gave you a quick answer, you might not continue praying for a project in the future. Quick answers might lead to superficial praying. Instead, God waits to test our resolve. The success of persistent prayer teaches us to be persistent the next time we pray.

We must pray long and we must pray with all our heart, because we are in spiritual warfare. The Christian life is not a coffee break; it's a wrestling match or a battlefield. Life's a struggle to the grave. There is an enemy, Satan, who opposes God's work; and when you are fasting and praying for a faith project, Satan opposes you. So keep praying. The issue is, "Who will win—God or Satan?" So you must pray through obstacles and pray through discouragement. Jesus encourages us, "Keep on praying and never give up" (Luke 18:1, *CEV*).

Paul reminds us, "For we do not wrestle against flesh and blood, but against principalities, against powers, against the rulers of the darkness of this age, against spiritual hosts of wickedness in the heavenly places" (Eph. 6:12). Therefore, severe, life-changing issues demand our complete dedication until the completion of our fast deadline. Remember, these are the vows you've made:

Abstinence-vow

Time-vow

Mental-vow

Prayer-vow

Faith-vow

Sometimes you pray long to undo the work of the enemy. Sometimes you pray long to give God time to put the pieces together so the answer can happen. If you're praying long for rain (see Jas. 5:17-18), it takes time for a weather front to come together and move through your area. If you're praying for money, it takes time to move a giver's heart to give and then write the check; and everyone laughs about the slow mail system.

Then again, remember that the *principle of learning* is tied to the *principle of time*. It takes time to learn some lessons, and the harder the lesson, the longer it takes to get ready for the exam. Have you ever studied almost all night to get ready for a final exam? Therefore, as you are praying through a 10- or 21-day fast, God may be trying to teach you an important lesson. It may take a whole 21 days to learn what God is teaching. And the lesson God wants to teach you may be something entirely different from the faith project.

Prevailing prayer is an attitude God teaches, so when you learn this lesson, determine to never give up. Make a vow now that you will keep your Daniel Fast to the end. Pray till you complete the vow you've made. Pray till you finish your Daniel Fast. Pray till you get an answer.

My Time to Pray

Lord, I confess my weakness; help me to be strong in this fast.

Lord, I've completed seven days; help me to keep my vow about not eating to the end, and help me pray persistently till the answer comes.

Lord, I commit the next days of my fast to You. Be glorified by my commitment and help me keep my promise. Amen.

My Answers Today

_____

_____

_____

_____

_____

_____

_____

_____

_____

_____

Note
1. Wesley L. Duwel, *Prevailing Prayer* (Grand Rapids, MI: Zondervan: 1990).

For suggested recipes, see pages 180-192.

Day 8 to Day 14 Overview

Learning About Prayer

These seven devotionals are written to teach you some basic lessons about prayer. In one sense, you don't need to learn to pray, for it's as basic as talking. But remember, you're talking to someone; prayer is relationship with God.

So, it's not always how you talk to God, or what you say to God; the key is relationship. Spend time with God, get to know Him and learn to worship Him.

This Daniel Fast could bring you closer to God than you've ever been in your life. Wouldn't you like that? Use prayer opportunities to get to know God intimately. Paul's great passion was, "That I may know Him and the power of His resurrection" (Phil. 3:10).

So don't forget to keep your fast vow, but more importantly, keep your prayer commitment. Jesus said, "Always pray and not lose heart" (Luke 18:1, *Phillips*).

Daily Readings

Day 8: Intimacy with God
Day 9: Giving Thanks in Prayer
Day 10: Fasting to Hunger After God
Day 11: Prayer Is Asking
Day 12: Fasting to Worship God
Day 13: Fasting to Locate Sin
Day 14: Don't Violate Your Fast

�֍ DAY 8 �֍

Intimacy with God

We tend to think of fasting as going without food. But we can fast from anything. If we love music and decide to miss a concert in order to spend time with God, that is fasting. It is helpful to think of the parallel of human friendship. When friends need to be together, they will cancel all other activities in order to make that possible. There's nothing illogical about fasting. It's just one way of telling God that your priority at that moment is to be alone with Him, sorting out whatever is necessary, and you have cancelled the meal, party, concert or whatever else you had planned to do in order to fulfill that priority.

J. I. PACKER

There are many ways to define prayer. Prayer is asking, and prayer is worshiping or praising God. Also, prayer is resting in God; or prayer is spiritual warfare against our enemy. But today, let's focus on intimacy in prayer. How intimate with God are you?

Look at the model of Jesus' life. He taught us to pray beginning with the words, "Our Father in heaven" (Matt. 6:9). Jesus invites us to enter into an intimate relationship with the heavenly Father, an intimacy that He shared with the Father.

The first recorded spoken words of Jesus occurred when He was 12 years old. Mary and Joseph had brought the family to Jerusalem for a feast. They had probably traveled in a large group and assumed Jesus was with them as they began returning home. But He was not. Mary and Joseph searched for a couple of days until they found Him in the Temple. When asked why, Jesus an-

swered, "Did you not know that I must be about My Father's business?" (Luke 2:49).

Many people read that story and emphasize that Jesus was in
the house of God. As good as that point is, the emphasis is that Jesus sought intimacy with God in His house. Jesus called God His
Father, a term of intimacy.

Look at Jesus' baptism. The Father showed up because it was
the inauguration of His Son into ministry. Don't fathers show up
for important days in the lives of their children? The heavenly Father said, "You are My beloved Son; in You I am well pleased"
(Luke 3:22).

Again when Jesus was transformed in front of three of His disciples on the Mount of Transfiguration, the Father spoke from
heaven, "This is My beloved Son, in whom I am well pleased"
(Matt. 17:5).

There is a difference between the relationship of a father with
his child and the reverence between a worshiper and God.

Relationship binds children to their father;
reverence binds worshipers to their God.

In the Old Testament, God revealed Himself by three names.
First, He revealed Himself as Elohim, God the powerful Creator
who called the world into existence. Second, He revealed Himself
as Yahweh (Jehovah), the personal LORD who told Moses, "I AM
WHO I AM" (Exod. 3:14). Third, He was Adonai, our master and
owner, and we are but slaves.

Not once in the Old Testament is God given the name Father
(seven times in the Gospel of John, Jesus says His name is Father).
In the Old Testament, God is likened to many things; for example,
He is likened to a rock (see Ps. 61:2; 2 Sam. 22:3), an eagle (see
Deut. 32:18; Ps. 139:8), a mother (see Pss. 17:8; 36:7; 57:1; 91:1,4)
and a father (see Eph. 3:15; Acts 17:24; Ps. 34:15-22). And here's
another example: "But now, O LORD, You are our Father; We are
the clay, and You our potter" (Isa. 64:8). Those are all metaphors
to help the people understand God.

Jesus taught His disciples that they had a new relationship with God. He taught them to pray, "Our Father in heaven" (Matt. 6:9). Because of Jesus, we have a new relationship with God, our heavenly Father.

The relationship between the Father and Jesus was revealed in a deeper intimacy when Jesus prayed in Gethsemane, "Abba, Father, all things are possible for You. Take this cup away from Me; nevertheless, not what I will, but what You will" (Mark 14:36). When Jesus called the Father, "Abba," it's like an American calling his father, "Papa."

The strength that Jesus got from that intimate relationship with His heavenly Father gave Him the ability to face the physical sufferings and the spiritual struggles on the cross when He became sin for us (see 2 Cor. 5:21).

What's satisfying about this relationship between Jesus and His heavenly Father? It reminds us of the intimate relationship between an earthly father and a child. The child runs to the arms of his father when returning from a trip and asks, "What did you bring me?" Is that a picture of you praying for your Daniel Fast project? For what are you asking?

Look at an exhausted child sitting in the lap of his father at a picnic. The child sleeps or rests quietly in his father's lap to regain strength to go play again. They don't need to say anything to each other; they just enjoy the moment. Dad's presence is good enough.

Can we pray without words? Yes! Remember, the most used word for prayer in the New Testament is *proseuchomai* (*pros* means "toward" and *euchomai* is "the face"). Prayer is like a face-to-face relationship with God that is pictured by two lovers sitting face to face, looking into one another's eyes; they don't need to say anything; their intimacy says, "I love you."

Intimacy is enjoying the presence of God. "David . . . sat before the LORD" (2 Sam. 7:18). When you come to your time of prayer, remember that you, too, can sit in the presence of the heavenly Father. Enjoy Him.

Because you are God's child, begin your prayers the way Paul taught us to approach the Father: "And because you are sons, God has sent forth the Spirit of His Son into your hearts, crying out, 'Abba, Father!'" (Gal. 4:6). What intimate name do you use for your heavenly Father?

In another Scripture, Paul taught us, "We are children of God, and if children, then heirs—heirs of God and joint heirs with Christ" (Rom. 8:16-17). Who is an heir? The one who has the right to the assets and property of the Father. So pray confidently in your Daniel Fast project. Ask as a child seeking assets from your heavenly Father.

Intimacy with God can seem mysterious. How can you be confident in your attempts to know God as you would your earthly father? There are several ways to define intimacy and the actions that lead to experiencing it with your heavenly Father.

First, intimacy is being there. You don't get intimacy with God by methods, techniques or even correct formulas in prayer. You get intimacy by drawing close to your heavenly Father. "How lovely is Your tabernacle, O LORD of hosts! My soul longs, yes, even faints For the courts of the LORD; My heart and my flesh cry out for the living God. For a day in Your courts is better than a thousand. I would rather be a doorkeeper in the house of my God than dwell in the tents of wickedness" (Ps. 84:1-2,10).

Second, intimacy is seeking the Father's presence. The Father is sitting on the throne of heaven. Why don't you go crawl up onto His lap? Just as a child on earth goes to sit with his or her earthly father, you can do the same with your heavenly Father.

And why does a child desire to sit on his father's lap? Maybe he wants to ask for something, or he wants his father to read to him. Maybe he needs help with homework. Perhaps the child just wants to sit in his father's lap because he enjoys it. Isn't intimacy wonderful? "One thing I have desired of the LORD, that will I seek: That I may dwell in the house of the LORD All the days of my life, To behold the beauty of the LORD, And to inquire in His temple" (Ps. 27:4).

Third, to experience intimacy with God, you don't need to learn anything. Kids don't need to take a course to learn how to be children. They just are. It comes with birth. When they are born into a family, they experience a father's love. That makes them know they are family. Love teaches them how to act and how to respond to their father. Love opens the door for them to ask.

Isn't it the role of a father to provide necessities—food, shelter, clothing—to his children? Yes. Isn't it the role of children to ask for necessities from their human father? Yes. So today, ask for your Daniel Fast project.

A kid sitting on his dad's lap doesn't need to take a course in how to be a kid. He just sits there and does what's natural. What's natural for you to do in your heavenly Father's presence?

Fourth, intimacy is a privilege to enjoy. I love the picture of President John F. Kennedy sitting for an important staff meeting when his son—John-John—bursts into the room and interrupts him. What happened? President Kennedy stopped what he was doing to set his son on his lap. At that moment, the request of his son was more important than any business of the United States.

When you burst into the throne room of heaven, God will stop what He's doing to listen to your request. At that moment, your request will be more important than God running the affairs of the universe.

Fifth, intimacy is learned from heaven, not earth. While I have discussed the intimacy between an earthly father and his children, that is not our model. Remember, some children had poor human role models in their fathers. Some fathers have been drunks, gamblers, and were lazy and abusive. So some people on earth have no good memory of a positive relationship with an earthly father.

In creation, God built the concept of fatherhood into men, and if they follow the inner directive, they'll become good fathers. But when earthly fathers give themselves to sin, they destroy the positive relationship they could have with their children and their children with them.

If your earthly experience makes prayers of intimacy with God difficult, ask God to heal your memories. Then ask God to heal your inclinations; and finally, ask Him to heal your lack of desire for intimacy with Him.

You must forgive any family members that have destroyed any idea of intimacy. Pray, "Forgive us our sins, just as we have forgiven those who have sinned against us" (Matt. 6:12, *TLB*).

Sixth, let intimacy develop. Some people just don't feel connected to God. How can they get past the "asking" phase of prayer to intimacy prayer? The simple answer is to give it time. Go into God's presence and wait.

The psalmist tells us, "Wait on the Lord" (Ps. 27:14). But make sure you are waiting in God's presence. "My soul, wait silently for God alone" (Ps. 62:5).

What happens when you wait on God? "Those who wait on the Lord shall renew their strength; They shall mount up with wings like eagles, They shall run and not be weary, They shall walk and not faint" (Isa. 40:31). So waiting on God gets results.

Seventh, expect to grow the art of intimacy. What do we know about babies? They are selfish. They expect everything from their parents, and if they don't get what they want when they want it, and in the way they want it, they will cry, scream and demand attention until they are satisfied. It's natural for babies to cry. Are you a baby in your relationship with God?

They cry for food until the bottle comes. They cry when a diaper is wet until they are changed. Some even cry when they feel ignored. Are you a spiritual baby? If so, cry to God for whatever you need.

Crying babies are not concerned if it's the middle of the night and their parents are sound asleep. They're not concerned if the pastor is preaching the Word of God and they disrupt a church service. No, babies are utterly selfish. Be careful that doesn't describe your prayer life.

But babies are not irreversibly selfish. As they grow, they learn better ways to express their needs. They learn to respect others and their needs. God has given a family to teach babies how to share, receive, give and love. The password to growth is love. "We love Him because He first loved us" (1 John 4:19).

Babies grow into mature adults in an atmosphere of love. With time they learn to give Dad a tie on Father's Day; and as they grow older, they give him respect and grow in relational intimacy with him.

Eighth, true intimacy balances the tension between reverence and relationship. God is the Creator of the universe; we reverence Him.

Because God is the omnipotent I AM WHO I AM, we bow in His presence to cry out, "Holy, Holy, Holy." That is the almighty side of the door.

But when we step through the door, we find ourselves in the presence of our heavenly Father—Abba Father—Papa. We can enter close up and metaphorically throw our arms around His neck and tell Him, "I love You."

My Time to Pray

Lord, I will wait in Your presence, not asking for anything.
I wait in Your presence to know You better.

Lord, I want to know You intimately, more intimately than
I know anyone on earth.

Lord, I reverence You as my sovereign Lord and the God of the universe.
I worship, adore and bow before You.

Lord, teach me when to reverence You and when to seek
Your intimacy. Amen.

My Answers Today

_____

_____

_____

_____

_____

_____

_____

_____

_____

_____

For suggested recipes, see pages 180-192.

❧ DAY 9 ❧

Giving Thanks in Prayer

A spiritually awake person would see everything as gift, even suffering. We deserve nothing and yet we so often act as though we deserve everything. Nothing should be taken for granted. We should say thank you every day to God and to each other for all that is provided for us.
This is one reason why fasting is such an important spiritual discipline. Not just fasting from food, but also fasting from cars, shopping centres, the new—whatever we have an inordinate attachment to. Fasting can help rekindle our gratitude for all that we have been given.

GLEN ARGAN

I meet with a group of about 12 people for prayer every Sunday morning. This is my most important meeting each week because I get more spiritual power and emotional energy from these people than from any other gathering.

Recently one person asked me, "Why do you always begin praying by thanking God for answers to your prayers?"

I had never thought about it; I didn't realize I began my prayers that way. So I asked, "How long have I been doing it?"

"Forever," he said.

Then I began to analyze why I did it that way. Maybe it's because my mother taught me to say thank you when someone gave me something or did something for me. But I think it is more than a habit.

Then I realized that I often repeat the statement, "Gratitude is the least remembered of all virtues and is the acid test of your character." Those who give thanks develop one of the greatest Christian virtues of all. Maybe I give thanks because it's part of my nature. Maybe I give thanks because I know God deserves my appreciation. And yes, maybe I give thanks for past answers because that's a foundation for future answers.

The word "thanksgiving" comes from *eucharisteo*. At the root of this word is *charis*, which is "grace." When you give someone thanks, you communicate "grace"; and in the process, you acquire grace.

The message of the New Testament is grace—it's God doing for you the exact opposite of what you deserve. You deserve hell, but you get heaven. You deserve alienation, but you get intimacy with God. You deserve punishment for your sins (we all do), but you get forgiveness and you get God's love.

To know God loves you is the greatest gift of grace. That knowledge demands thankfulness. When you experience grace, you can do nothing but give thanks to the Giver of grace.

Why Give Thanks?

First, a thankful heart to God puts you on praying ground. So approach God with a grateful heart for everything He's given you. Then He will recognize your sincerity and listen. God will realize you are not bragging, nor are you self-centered. A thankful heart makes you focus on God, and that puts you on praying ground next to the heart of God.

Paul gives us the example of approaching God with a thankful heart: "Now thanks be to God who always leads us in triumph in Christ, and through us diffuses the fragrance of His knowledge in every place" (2 Cor. 2:14).

Then Paul instructs us to attach thanksgiving to our prayers. "In everything by prayer and supplication, with thanksgiving, let your requests be made known to God" (Phil. 4:6). Did you notice that "thanksgiving" comes before making "your requests known to God"?

Second, a thankful heart is an obedient heart. We are commanded to give thanks to God in the psalms: "Give thanks to the LORD!" (see Pss. 30:4; 97:12; 105:1; 106:1,47; 107:1; 118:1,29; 136:1,2,3,26).

Paul also instructed us to tie thanksgiving to our prayers: "Continue earnestly in prayer, being vigilant in it with thanksgiving" (Col. 4:2). He probably told us to give thanks because it was his habit in prayer (see Rom. 1:8; 1 Cor. 1:4; Phil. 1:3; 1 Thess. 2:13; 2 Thess. 1:3; 1 Tim. 1:12; 2 Tim. 1:3; Philem. v. 4).

Since you are instructed to give God thanks, why not do it? And if you obediently give thanks, don't you think God will realize what you're doing and listen to your request?

Third, a thankful heart stimulates your faith to trust God again for another answer to prayer and for even greater answers to prayer. When Daniel was persecuted for his faith, and a civic law was passed that prohibited his prayer life, Daniel didn't quit praying. But he began his prayer with thanksgiving:

"Now when Daniel knew that the writing was signed, he went home. And in his upper room, with his windows open toward Jerusalem, he knelt down on his knees three times that day, and prayed and gave thanks before his God, as was his custom since early days" (Dan. 6:10). Because Daniel knew God had answered his prayers in the past, he began praying—perhaps the most important prayer of his life—with thanksgiving.

Fourth, a thankful prayer or attitude will be a testimony to others. When Paul was instructing the Colossians on how to live for Christ, he told them, "And let the peace of God rule in your hearts, to which also you were called in one body; and be thankful" (Col. 3:15).

It appears that inward peace of the heart and outward thanksgiving are tied together. If we are thankful for our spouse and children, we don't criticize and desire better. If we are thankful for all the "stuff" in our life, we won't break the tenth commandment, "You shall not covet . . ." (Exod. 20:17).

Fifth, thanksgiving is a synonym for praise and blessing. It's one of the ways to worship God. When you thank God for all that you are and all you have and all that God's done for you, you put Him first. Your life centers on God, and not on yourself.

We are instructed, "Enter into His gates with thanksgiving, And into His courts with praise. Be thankful to Him, and bless

His name" (Ps. 100:4). So, what must be our attitude when we appreciate God with worship?

We give Him thanks!

How can we offer praise to God?

We give Him thanks!

How is the best way to bless God?

We give Him thanks!

Sixth, the example of Jesus. The one person who didn't need to give thanks to the heavenly Father was His Son, Jesus Christ. The Father and Son are equal in nature, so the Son didn't need to give thanks; but He did.

Notice what Jesus did before feeding 5,000 with five fishes and two barley loaves. He gave thanks: "And Jesus took the loaves, and when He had given thanks He distributed them to the disciples, and the disciples to those sitting down; and likewise of the fish, as much as they wanted" (John 6:11).

Inasmuch as Jesus came to earth as a Jew and lived a perfect life, He would have given thanks as did those Jews who wanted to be perfect in God's sight.

We should be thankful because of Jesus' example of thankfulness. Remember, Peter said that you "should follow His steps" (1 Pet. 2:21). Since Jesus continually gave thanks, how could we do otherwise?

Seventh, thanksgiving stirs our memory of Christ's death. Some Christian groups call the Communion service the Eucharist. That word comes from *eucharisteo*, which means "giving thanks." The focus of the Lord's Table is that the partakers give thanks for all that Christ did on the cross.

In looking forward to His death, Jesus initiated giving thanks: "And He took bread, gave thanks and broke it, and gave it to them, saying, 'This is My body which is given for you; do this in remembrance of Me'" (Luke 22:19). So we eat with thanksgiving.

Then Jesus took the cup and repeated the same formula: "Then He took the cup, and gave thanks, and gave it to them, saying, 'Drink from it, all of you'" (Matt. 26:27).

I was pastor of Faith Bible Church in Dallas, Texas, from 1956 to 1958. They celebrated the Communion service after the pattern of the old Moravians or the Plymouth Brethren Assemblies. The entire service was spent around the Communion service.

I would ask one of the brethren, "Would you thank God for the broken body of Jesus for your sins?" I would follow by asking several more brethren to pray the same prayer. Then the bread was passed and we all ate together.

Then we followed the same pattern for the cup. Several were asked, "Would you thank God for that spilt blood of Jesus for your sins?"

We are as close to God as we can get when we come to Him in thanksgiving for His broken body and spilt blood.

My Time to Pray

Lord, for all the "great things You have done" (Ps. 126:2, ELT), thank You.

Lord, for answered prayers in the past, thank You.

Lord, for protection from known and unknown dangers, thank You.
Lord, for guidance to do Your will, and Your patience with me when I haven't done Your will, thank You.

Lord, for saving me and giving me Your assurance in dark days, thank You.

Lord, for all Christ did for me on Calvary, thank You.

Lord, I thank You for Your awesome majesty and lovingkindness to me. Amen.

My Answers Today

_____
_____
_____
_____
_____
_____
_____
_____
_____

For suggested recipes, see pages 180-192.

❧ DAY 10 ❧

Fasting to Hunger After God

Bear up the hands that hang down, by faith and prayer; support the tottering knees. Have you any days of fasting and prayer? Storm the throne of grace and persevere therein, and mercy will come down.

JOHN WESLEY

I had been fasting for several days, and it was going well. Bill Greig, Jr., the president of Gospel Light Publishing, asked me, "What great answer to prayer have you gotten because of your fast?"

"I'm not fasting to get an answer to prayer," was my immediate response.

"Then why are you putting yourself through all this torture if you're not fasting to get an answer to prayer?"

"I'm fasting to know God intimately," I said. "My fast is not about getting things from God. I'm fasting to experience God more intimately."

"Oh . . . write that for Regal Books. That's an enticing topic for a book."

I went straight up to my hotel room and began writing what was eventually to be published with the title *God Encounters*.[1]

Even though Bill was right in saying "knowing God" is a worthy topic for a book, Bill was wrong on two other things: First, he asked why I was putting myself through all this trouble. A lot of non-fasters think fasting is difficult or hurtful, or those fasting suffer misery and mental torture. Bill, just like a lot of people facing a fast, thought it was "no fun" or a "torturous experience."

When you spend time with God, it's a satisfying experience. Those who are meeting God experience deep joy. It's an intimacy that's hard to describe or put into words. (More about that later in this chapter.)

Bill was also wrong in thinking that fasting is only about getting answers to prayer. Oh yes, fasting does get answers to prayer. Remember, Jesus told us, "However, this kind does not go out except by prayer and fasting" (Matt. 17:21). But fasting is more than a physical activity of withholding food; we fast *and* pray to get God's attention.

Now, you're on a Daniel Fast and you may be praying for a project at your church, or some personal goal. You're probably following a modified diet and you're spending time in prayer. But in this chapter, let's turn our attention away from the project or goal of your Daniel Fast. Let's examine what happens to your fellowship with God when you fast.

Stay in the Moment

The body is a great big engine. We know that all engines need fuel, whether the fuel is gas, coal, wood or some other type of energy-producing fuel. So our body also needs food to produce the tremendous amount of energy we expend each day. Sometimes, the more energy we expend, the more fuel (calories—carbohydrates, fats and protein) we need to keep going.

When your car is almost out of gas, it begins to skip and cough to tell you it's about to stall. In the same way, if you are used to eating three meals a day—then you miss three meals—your stomach will let you know it's time for a refill.

I don't want to worry you, but during the first 20 days of a fast, you live off the fat in your body by burning it away. (Your fat is the energy to run your body.) That's good because disease is circulated in your body by the blood but finally is deposited in your fat. In a fast, you get rid of potential disease. Maybe that's why God told the

Jews in the Old Testament not to eat the fat or drink the blood (see Lev. 6:26; 7:24-25). Maybe God's instructions were *preventative health* to keep Israel physically free from physical disease and physical weaknesses. So fasting is good—not harmful—because you purge your physical body from potential sickness and disease.

So when you don't eat—because you're fasting—you get signals from your body on a regular basis, "feed me." Every signal should remind you of the purpose of your Daniel Fast. Every time your stomach "growls" or "gurgles," you are reminded that "this fast is for God."

Hunger pangs should keep you in a
God-inspired moment.

But it's not just your stomach that sends you messages. Every billboard on the highway seems to advertise hamburgers, pizza or some snack. I never remembered seeing so many of these signals until I fasted for 40 days.

Also the TV screen is your enemy. Commercials fill the screen with juicy steaks or luscious cooked lobster prepared to perfection and seasoned perfectly. And it's never a random camera shot of a plate of food; the steak or lobster fills the screen to the edges.

When these mental images of food come, that's a great time to apply spiritual discipline and pray. Rather than thinking about food, or lusting for food, I pray for my project and the goal for which I'm fasting. It's one thing to hunger for food; it's a greater thing to hunger for God's presence in your life.

Jesus said that God would bless—add value—to the one who hungered for God, because the word "bless" means "to add value." Jesus promised, "Blessed are those who hunger and thirst for righteousness, for they shall be filled" (Matt. 5:6). Did you take note of the promise "They shall be filled"? When you're really hungry for a hot, juicy hamburger from your favorite place, there's no satisfaction like sitting down to slowly munch it down.

In the same way, there are times when you really want God to manifest Himself to you. You need God, and You want Him with all your heart. Fasting from earthly food is one way to find God's presence.

The longer you fast, the more keen your thinking becomes. You're not consumed with feeding your body. God begins to consume your thinking—all your experiences. You focus on Him alone. You cry out, "That I may know Him" (Phil. 3:10).

It's not just your mental processes that focus on God when you fast. The brain thinks more clearly and you remember more when fasting. Perhaps it's because your heart is not pumping extra blood to your stomach to digest food. There is extra blood available to the brain, and more blood means the brain functions better.

That's why ginkgo biloba stimulates your mind and helps you remember. It's an herb that increases blood to the brain. So you think clearer when fasting. Therefore, focus your mind on Jesus.

The psalmist exhorts us, "Oh, taste and see that the LORD is good" (Ps. 34:8). When you refrain from earthly food, you can enjoy heavenly food; you fill yourself with Christ alone.

Jesus called Himself bread: "I am the bread of life. He who comes to Me shall never hunger" (John 6:35). We eat for strength and for life; but God also gave us the gift of food to enjoy. Doesn't food satisfy us? Cool, crispy watermelon on a hot humid day! Hot, steaming pizza on a cool evening! Sizzling steak when we're extra hungry! So think of the satisfaction we get from Jesus when we bring our empty heart to Him.

Jesus gives satisfying life, for He promised, "He who comes to Me shall never hunger" (John 6:35). As we fast, we find that Jesus fills every yearning of the heart.

Many have misunderstood Jesus' sermon on the bread of life. He promised, "Unless you eat the flesh of the Son of Man and drink His blood, you have no life in you. Whoever eats My flesh and drinks My blood has eternal life, and I will raise him up at the last day" (John 6:53-54). Some have wrongly thought Christians were cannibals who stole the body of Jesus and ate it. Others have said they must eat and drink of the Lord's Table to be saved. Both ideas are wrong.

When Jesus told us to eat and drink of Himself, it had to do with our union with Christ. When we got saved, we invited Jesus to live in our hearts, and He entered our earthly life to give us eternal life. It's a picture of eating a sandwich that enters our body to give us strength to continue living.

Yes, when we fast, we focus on Jesus who lives within. As we read the Scriptures, we take Christ into our life anew, for Jesus is "the Word [of God]" (John 1:1). So read much Scripture when you are fasting. The Bible—Jesus' words—renews our will to live for God and sharpens our mind to think on God.

That leads us to the second step; if the first step is *union*, then the second step is *communion*. You will have deeper fellowship, or communion, with Christ during a fast than at any other time. Your fast ought to produce union *and* communion.

Let's look at another verse where Jesus tells us to eat of Himself. This one promises us *union and communion*: "He who eats My flesh and drinks My blood abides in Me, and I in him" (John 6:56).

When Jesus says, "I in Him," that's when we have union with Christ. This is the union that begins at salvation because we take Christ into our heart (see John 7:12; Eph. 5:17). We are united to Christ by salvation. So where is Christ when you fast? He's living in your heart.

The other part of that verse, "abides in me," means that we have fellowship, or communion, with Christ. So when you are fasting, you ought to be closer to God than any other time during your Christian experience.

I remember once during a fast attending my church's evening candlelight Communion service. I had not eaten for more than 20 days and was not at all hungry. I hadn't even thought that the Communion service involved eating the bread. I didn't realize I had a problem until the deacon took the white covering off the elements. Then the question hit me, "Shall I eat the Communion bread?"

I was at day 20, heading to a 40-day fast. I was fasting to God and wanted Him to be glorified in all I did.

I rationalized, *I can drink the cup because I'm drinking orange juice every morning.* But no solid food had entered my mouth. Then I thought, *I won't eat the bread. I don't care what others think if I don't eat the bread; this is private between God and me.*

I decided not to eat the bread and drink the cup. I would keep my fast "perfectly" to God. I would pray and meditate as others took Communion. I even wrongly thought, *It would be better if I hadn't come to church tonight so I could honor my fast in private.* Then it dawned on me: *Eating the bread is a picture of communion with Christ; so is fasting when I don't eat.*

So I ate the bread wafer that evening as I fellowshipped with Christ who dwelt in my heart. From that moment on I didn't feel as if I was violating my fast. If anything, I was enhancing my fast because I was communing with Christ, which was one of the purposes of the fast.

My Time to Pray

Lord, I want to know You more intimately as I proceed in this Daniel Fast.

Lord, reveal Yourself to me as I seek to know You.

Lord, I confess my carnality and lack of love to You. Forgive me for being shallow; take me deep with You.

Lord, I commit myself in this Daniel Fast to know You better than I've ever known You in my life. Amen.

My Answers Today

_____

_____

_____

_____

_____

_____

_____

Note
1. Elmer L. Towns, *God Encounters* (Ventura, CA: Regal Books, 2000).

For suggested recipes, see pages 180-192.

❧ DAY 11 ❧

Prayer Is Asking

Fasting is not confined to abstinence from eating and drinking.
Fasting really means voluntary abstinence for a time from various necessities
of life such as food, drink, sleep, rest, association with people and so forth. The
purpose of such abstinence for a longer period or shorter period of time is to
loosen to some degree the ties which bind us to the world or material things
and our surroundings as a whole, in order that we may concentrate all our
spiritual powers upon the unseen and eternal things.

O. HALLESBY

We come to an interesting question: Why does God want His children to ask Him for things? Isn't God all-knowing? Doesn't He already know our needs? And didn't Jesus say, "Your Father knows
the things you have need of before you ask Him" (Matt. 6:8)? So
why go without eating as you pray?

Because prayer is relationship with God, have you ever thought
of the possibility that God wants to spend time with you? Perhaps
that's the reason God gives us the opportunity to ask Him questions. He wants us to spend time with Him.

The fourteen-time Grammy Award winner Ricky Skaggs read
my book *Fasting for Spiritual Breakthrough* and sent word he wanted
to spend the day with me just to learn about fasting and prayer. So
I spent a Wednesday in September 2007 with him.

Sir Edmund Hillary, the first man to climb Mount Everest,
read the same book and sent word he wanted to chat with me
about fasting. I was making plans to travel to New Zealand to have
tea with him, but he died before I could meet with him.

If famous people want to talk to you about fasting, you would probably rearrange your calendar to make it happen. But God is greater than any famous person. Now you've rearranged your schedule to talk with God as you fast. Your Daniel Fast could produce your greatest conversation in history; you're going to talk with the LORD of the universe.

But you're doing more than talking to God about your prayer project. You're altering your diet for 10 or 21 days so that you can ask God for something that's special, and to you, probably very necessary.

Asking is an elementary form of dependence on God. When you ask your mother-in-law for advice, doesn't that show you trust her, and doesn't that draw the two of you closer together? Now you've honored God by asking for answers to your prayer. It shows you believe He can do the thing for which you are asking.

Asking puts you in partnership with God. When you ask someone to help you with a project, doesn't that mean the two of you will work together? Then think of how close you get to a friend when you ask him or her to pray with you about a need (see Matt. 18:19). How close does it put you with God when you ask for His help?

One more thing: You should ask because God likes to be asked. That's why Jesus told us to ask (see Matt. 7:7-8). Don't parents enjoy it when their children ask them for something? Sure! Parents probably already know what their kids need—and maybe even what their kids are wishing to get. And doesn't it make a parent feel good to know their children think they can get anything for them? Love grows in a relationship of asking and getting.

I take my grandchildren—and their parents—out to eat on Sundays after church at an Italian restaurant we all love. Nearby is a Dollar Store where everything costs $1. I take the children there after eating and say, "You can have anything you want!"

They go wild running the aisles, trying to find what they want most. Two of my grandchildren, whose mother is a strict disciplinarian, will only ask for one thing a week. Another grandchild lives only with his mother, who doesn't have much. He at first wanted two or three items. Then, five or six. Finally, it got up to 10 to 12.

What's a couple of dollars, I thought, *compared to the joy we both get out of this experience?*

So that leads to fellowship. When we ask something of God, it enriches our fellowship with our Father. We tell Him what we want, and we get as close to Him as possible to deepen our relationship so we'll get what we need.

And don't forget memories. I take my grandchildren to the Dollar Store to create pleasant memories about their grandfather. So every time you get something from God, you remember a previous answer to prayer and it motivates you to ask again and again; and of course you keep in good relationship with God so you'll get it again and again.

I can still see this little fella who gets 10 or 12 items. He'll come and stand by my chair as I finish my spaghetti and meatballs or Philly cheese steak sandwich. He doesn't say anything; he just stands there. I know what he wants, so I quickly finish and we go to the Dollar Store. You know I love it! So go stand near your heavenly Father and wait for the answer you seek.

Asking in Jesus' Name

Jesus told His disciples, "Until now you have asked nothing in My name" (John 16:24). He was introducing them to a new relationship of asking-prayer from the Father. After Jesus died and went to heaven, His followers would have a new and different prayer relationship with Him.

What was that new prayer relationship? "Ask, and you will receive, that your joy may be full" (John 16:24). That part about joy means Jesus was saying, "You're going to be happy when I answer your prayers" (John 16:24, *ELT*).

Jesus was not using His name as some sort of mantra, nor was it a secret code that opened locked things, or a magical key to open doors. When Jesus said to "[ask] in My name," He wasn't even telling us to add His name to the end of our prayers to get things from the Father, although we do end our prayers in Jesus' name.

To pray in Jesus' name is to take full advantage of His death to take away our sins (see John 1:29). Because His blood cleanses us from every sin in our life (see 1 John 1:7), His death sealed our eternal relationship with the Father. So every time we pray in Jesus' name, we take advantage of what He did on the cross to connect us to our heavenly Father.

But there's also a present relationship. When we pray in Jesus' name, we identify with Jesus' new life in heaven. More than 172 times in the New Testament we are said to be "in Christ." We are as close to the Father's heart as Jesus. So ask what you need "in Jesus' name"; He has promised to hear and answer. Paul tells us about this new relationship:

> But God, who is rich in mercy, because of His great love with which He loved us, even when we were dead in trespasses, made us alive together with Christ (by grace you have been saved), and raised us up together, and made us sit together in the heavenly places in Christ Jesus (Eph. 2:4-6).

One more thing about praying in Jesus' name: He's in your heart! You asked Him to come into your life when you got saved. Paul prayed for the Ephesians to understand their new relationship that "Christ may dwell in your heart through faith" (Eph. 3:17). So ask in Jesus' name because He's in your heart.

Conditions

Obviously, you can't ask for just anything, nor will you get everything you ask for in prayer. God doesn't do impossible things like making the past never happen. You can't ask God to take away the abortion that you wish you had never had.

God won't give you something that will hurt you, or something you shouldn't have. Take for example my little grandson who likes to get a lot of things at the Dollar Store. I wouldn't buy him a new motorcycle or a new pair of $200 wingtip shoes. He can't use them, and he's not ready for them.

In the same vein, I wouldn't buy something that would hurt him—marijuana or a beer or a pack of cigarettes.

One Sunday the little guy wanted a pack of poker chips wrapped in a tube of cellophane—I wouldn't buy them, maybe because poker chips are a symbol for gambling. I walked him over to the cookie shelf and said, "I've got something better for you." Instead of a cellophane pack of poker chips, it was a cellophane pack of chocolate cookies. He smiled and was happy.

I thought of Elijah in the desert, sitting under a willow tree, weeping. He prayed to die, "LORD, take my life" (1 Kings 19:4). But God was smiling out on the darkness because He had something better for Elijah. I can hear God say, "How about a chariot and horses of fire? How about not dying at all?"

Next time you ask for something, and God says no, maybe He has got some chocolate cookies wrapped in cellophane, instead of poker chips.

The first condition of prayer in Jesus' name is to *ask*. That's it! Prayer is as simple as asking. You can keep your prayers on the lofty heights of worship and praise—ways to pray that are necessary—but if you don't ask, you may not get what you need.

Didn't James reinforce that method of praying? "You do not have because you do not ask" (Jas. 4:2). So maybe you haven't got the things(s) for which you are fasting because you haven't asked in the right way or with the right attitude or at the right time.

The second condition is to ask repeatedly or continually. Remember, Jesus said, "Keep on asking and it will be given you; keep on seeking and you will find; keep on knocking fervently and the door will be opened to you. For everyone who keeps on asking receives; and he who keeps on seeking finds; and to him who keeps on knocking, the door will be opened" (Matt. 7:7-8, ELT).

Is God telling you to pester Him? No! When God tells us to continually ask, He is telling us to keep our faith in Him strong. Sometimes God waits to see if we are sincere. At other times He begins to answer, but it takes time to get the answer to you. Maybe God wants you to keep on praying because He's going to slowly unfold the answer to you. Sometimes, the longer you pray the more of the answer you get.

If prayer is like the gasoline that runs the motor, maybe you need to pray often, like when I had to fill a very small gas tank on a small green lawnmower that I bought at a garage sale. I've never seen another lawn mower like that little thing. It would take four or five tanks of fuel to cut my lawn. Sometimes you have to keep putting prayer in to continue to get answers out.

A third condition is abiding in Christ, the living Word of God. He said, "If you abide in Me, and My words abide in you, you will ask what you desire, and it shall be done for you" (John 15:7). Usually, people think abiding means meditating on Christ or communing with Christ. It means that, but it also has a more elementary meaning. Abiding means obeying His commandments or rules. "He who keeps His commandments abides in Him" (1 John 3:24).

So the third condition deals with obedience. At another place in Scripture, John tells us, "Whatever we ask we receive from Him, because we keep His commandments" (1 John 3:22). As a kid, I knew I had to obey my mother if I wanted her to make some chocolate fudge or a churn of ice cream.

Why is it that we think we can curse with the Lord's name or fulfill our lust, or have illegal sex, or disobey our parents and still expect God to answer our prayers? Those who are the most obedient get the most answers.

What does it mean to let the words of Jesus, or the Bible, abide in you? It means you fill your life with Scripture. You go to church to hear the Bible preached and taught. You read it privately; you memorize it and meditate on it (see Ps. 1:1-3). You fill your life with the written Word of God, which is like filling your life with Jesus, the living Word of God.

When you live by the Scriptures, you are living a life that qualifies for answers to prayer. When the Bible controls your life, you don't ask for selfish things. You don't arbitrarily ask for $1,000,000 to make you happier or to fulfill any wish list you may conceive. When you are filled with the Bible, it controls your desires so that you want what God wants. Those who are controlled by the Bible will more likely pray according to the will of God.

That leads us to the fourth condition. We must pray according to God's will. John promised, "Now this is the confidence that we have in Christ, that when we ask for anything according to His will,

He hears us, and we know that we will get the petitions we ask of Him" (1 John 5:14-15, *ELT*).

Notice the progression in God's promises in 1 John 5:14-15. First, we ask according to God's will; second, we know that God hears us when we ask in His will; and third, we know we will receive the petitions we request from Him.

Remember the rock song of the 1960s sung by Janis Joplin? "Lord, won't you buy me a Mercedes, all my friends have Porsches."[1] Can we really think the will of God is a mansion in Beverly Hills or the most expensive luxury car or winning the lottery? No! You must pray within God's will to get answers.

God keeps many of His children on short financial leashes because if they had all the money they desired, or asked, they would winter in Palm Springs and summer on the French Riviera. Fulfilling the lust of the flesh (physical satisfaction) or the lust of the eye (things) or the pride of life (position or fame) would destroy them (see 1 John 2:15-17).

The fifth condition is faith. "But without faith it is impossible to please Him, for he who comes to God must believe that He is, and that He is a rewarder of those who diligently seek Him" (Heb. 11:6). To get your reward you must believe that God exists, then diligently seek Him for the petitions you want. Isn't that why you are fasting for 10 or 21 days?

Jesus told us to "have faith in God" (Mark 11:22). Then He told us we can exercise our faith by speaking words. This is what we do in prayer, "For assuredly, I say to you, whoever says to this mountain, 'Be removed and be cast into the sea,' and does not doubt in his heart, but believes that those things he says will be done, he will have whatever he says" (Mark 11:23). Did you see the word "says" three times in that verse? That means you are to *say* in faith what you want to receive in prayer. So tell God right now about the faith project for which you are fasting.

So, the fifth secret to getting answers to prayer is faith. After Jesus directed us to exercise faith, He told us how to do it: "Therefore I say to you, whatever things you ask when you pray, believe that you receive them, and you will have them" (Mark 11:24).

Aren't you diligently seeking God by fasting and prayer for an extended period of time? Didn't you begin the Daniel Fast as a statement of faith that you believe God could give you the faith project for which you pray? The more time you spend in prayer, and the longer you fast, the stronger your faith becomes.

Faith is believing God will hear you and that He will answer. Faith is a growing experience: "From faith to faith . . . the just shall live by faith" (Rom. 1:17). If you have beginning faith to start a fast, then the more you pray, the stronger your faith becomes.

The sixth condition deals with your life's fruit. The prayers we seek from God are tied to the fruit in our lives. We are told to abide in Jesus to have fruit: "He who abides in Me, and I in him, bears much fruit" (John 15:5).

Then Jesus promises, "I chose you and appointed you that you should go and bear fruit, and that your fruit should remain, that whatever you ask the Father in My name He may give you" (John 15:16). Here Jesus ties answers to prayer with fruit-bearing in our lives.

We have discussed six conditions to pray in Jesus' name. We can get our prayers answered because of the *friendship factor*. Don't we enjoy giving things to our friends when they ask? Jesus said, "You are My friends if you do whatever I command you" (John 15:14). When we are in fellowship with Jesus, and we walk with Him in friendship, isn't that the place where prayers get answered?

My Time to Pray

Lord, I believe You exist; You've saved me, and You answer prayer;
so come answer the prayer for which I'm fasting.

Lord, I know Jesus came into my heart and He lives in my life;
now I come through Jesus for the prayer project for which I'm fasting.

Lord, Jesus is sitting at Your right hand in glory, and I am positionally
"in Him." Now I come through Christ to get answers for which I am fasting.

Lord, give me faith to believe You for the answer for which I am fasting.
"I believe, help Thou my unbelief." Amen.

My Answers Today

_____

_____

_____

_____

_____

_____

_____

_____

_____

_____

_____

_____

_____

_____

Note

1. See Janis Joplin Lyrics, http://www.google.com/search?hl=en&q=Lord%2C+won%27t +you+buy+me+a+Mercedes&rlz=1W1GZEZ_en&aq=f&oq=&aqi=g4 (accessed June 18, 2009).

For suggested recipes, see pages 180-192.

❦ DAY 12 ❦

Fasting to Worship God

It is not wrong to fast, if we do it in the right way and with the right motive. Jesus fasted (Matt. 4:3); so did the members of the early church (Acts 13:2). Fasting helps to discipline the appetites of the body (Luke 21:34) and keep our spiritual priorities straight. But fasting must never become an opportunity for temptation (1 Cor. 7:7). Simply to deprive ourselves of a natural benefit (such as food or sleep) is not of itself fasting. We must devote ourselves to God and worship Him. Unless there is the devotion of heart (see Zech. 7) there is not lasting benefit.

WARREN W. WIERSBE

Have you ever asked yourself why you should worship God when He has all the angels of heaven worshiping Him? After all, they cry continually, "Holy, holy, holy is the LORD of hosts; the whole earth is full of His glory!" (Isa. 6:3).

It would seem that the praise they offer to God is far better than any praise that we could give Him. Why? Because angels can't sin, so they worship Him with a pure heart. Also, they are not influenced by selfishness and duplicity; nor do their thoughts tend to wander when they're praying. That means angels are not influenced by earthly desires, as we are, when they worship.

Another thing, angels worship God constantly: "They do not rest day or night, saying: 'Holy, holy, holy, Lord God Almighty, Who was and is and is to come!' " (Rev. 4:8). But we don't worship God continually, because we are busy earning money or looking after our family or doing 101 other things that crowd into our schedule.

And don't angels know more about God than we know about God? They stand in God's presence as ministering spirits for Him (see Heb. 1:14).

So this brings up an interesting question: Since God has a multitude of angels to worship Him continually, and they are more pure than we are, and they know more about God than we will know on this earth, why does He need our worship at all?

Technically, worship is the only thing that God can't do for Himself. If I write my own press release, brag about my accomplishments and boast to everyone how great I am, who would believe me? Doesn't Scripture say, "And a man is valued by what others say of him" (Prov. 27:21)?

But doesn't God already know His greatness and what He can do? So if God were to praise Himself, would it accomplish any heavenly good? God can't worship Himself; He wants us to be authentic worshipers. So from a sincere heart, Jesus told us, "The Father seeks worship" (John 4:23, *ELT*). So God seeks worship from His people to manifest all the things that He is and that He can do.

In Psalm 103, David wrote, "Bless the LORD, O my soul; And all that is within me, bless His holy name!" (Ps. 103:1). First, this teaches us to approach God with all our heart; that means nothing is held back or nothing is hidden from His view. Shouldn't we be openhearted in worshiping God? He knows all that we are and do, so we should be honest in our worship of Him.

Second, when we bless God, we add value to Him just as when we bless someone on this earth we add value to him or her. The word "bless" means "to add value" to something. I can bless my grandson financially by giving him money. I can bless my wife emotionally by serving her coffee in bed every morning when she wakes. We bless people spiritually when we help them learn the Bible or follow God's commandments.

So how can we bless God? He doesn't need our money; He doesn't need any of the stuff that we can give Him; we can't do anything to make His life easier. We can't give God anything He doesn't have. God needs absolutely nothing.

But when we bless the Lord, we give Him something He does not already have. We are adding value to God's kingdom by praising Him for redeeming our soul and transforming our life. We recognize God's goodness for saving us, and His greatness for giving us eternal life.

When we worship God, we move out of ourselves and get closer to Him, perhaps closer than ever before. We move away from our prayers and our petitions, and we focus on Him and His glory. When we worship God, we are not asking for something for ourselves, nor are we asking to get out of trouble or for Him to protect us. Our worship has nothing to do with ourselves; it has everything to do with God.

Why Praise God?

Have you ever noticed that we are commanded to worship God? The writer of Hebrews says, "Let us continually offer the sacrifice of praise to God, that is, the fruit of our lips, giving thanks to His name" (Heb. 13:15). Just as a peach tree produces peaches, so our mouths must produce the words of gratitude that come from our hearts because we are thankful that God has saved us.

But there's another reason to worship God. Let's think about what worship does for us. Each of us needs hope in this life for something outside ourselves. When we praise God for His protection over our life, we are lifted higher and closer to God than ever before. And isn't thankfulness great, because it keeps us from being pessimistic where we expect failure.

Worship keeps us from becoming bogged down in the depressing circumstances of life. Worship focuses our life on something greater than our present limitations. Praise keeps us from being self-centered and negative.

Think about what worship teaches us. Every time we praise God, we begin to learn something more about God—what He has done for us, and what He has promised He will do for us in the future. And as we learn more and more of what He has done for us, it deepens our relationship with Him.

Maybe this is why the disciples "were continually in the temple praising and blessing God" (Luke 24:53), and why Paul dedicated the book of Ephesians "to the praise and glory of His grace" (Eph. 1:6).

Practicing Worship

We can never achieve the highest level of praise like the angels worship God, yet we can pray with David, "Let the words of my mouth and the meditation of my heart be acceptable in Your sight" (Ps. 19:14). Although we can't pray in the words of angels, we can pray in the words of David and ask God to accept our daily praise.

Think of all the great things God does for you. It wouldn't hurt to make a list of all the things God has done for you and audibly repeat them in appreciation to God. Paul told us, "In everything by prayer and supplication, with thanksgiving, let your requests be made known to God" (Phil. 4:6); so we ought to use thanksgiving as a tool to help us pray better in the future.

Then we should do as David suggests: "Magnify the LORD . . . And let us exalt His name together" (Ps. 34:3). Look at that word "magnify"; it's impossible to magnify God because He can't get any bigger or any more awesome. So how do we magnify God? Think of your reading glasses. I need "cheaters" to read the gray newspaper and telephone book. When I use my "cheaters," the words are not magnified on the paper. We all know the words don't get any bigger. The words are magnified in my eyes to read better.

So when you magnify God, He becomes larger in your head and heart. And what do you do when that happens? You respond to God in a bigger or better way. You become absorbed into God and now you are ready to add prayers to your Daniel Fast.

Practice the continual presence of God in your life. David said, "I will bless the LORD at all times; His praise shall continually be in my mouth" (Ps. 34:1). As you go through this day, consciously look for the little ways that you see God in your life. Say a short prayer of thanksgiving for everything He does. The more you thank God for what He is doing in your life, the more His presence will be manifested in your life.

My Time to Pray

Lord, I will worship You from the bottom of my heart and I will not hold back any part of myself in my worship.

Lord, I will continually bless Your name and worship You in the big and little things of my life.

Lord, forgive me when I haven't seen Your presence in my life; when I am unaware of Your working in my life. Help me see more clearly as You develop Your will for my life, and teach me to be thankful for what You are doing.

Lord, thank You for revealing Yourself to me. Amen.

My Answers Today

_____
_____
_____
_____
_____
_____
_____
_____
_____
_____
_____
_____
_____
_____
_____
_____
_____
_____
_____

For suggested recipes, see pages 180-192.

❧ DAY 13 ❧

Fasting to Locate Sin

*Although there are many different kinds of fasts, the most common,
and the one I recommend for starting, is to abstain from food, but not drink,
for a given period of time. So far as drink is concerned, all agree that
water is basic. Some add coffee or tea; some add fruit juices.
All also agree that something like a milkshake goes too far and is not in the
spirit of fasting. Whatever, the fast involves an intentional practice of self-
denial, and this spiritual discipline has been known through the
centuries as a means for opening ourselves to God and drawing closer
to Him. . . . To the degree that fasting becomes more of a norm in our day-
to-day Christian life as individuals and congregations, we will
become more effective in spiritual warfare.*

C. PETER WAGNER

In October 1973, the students of Liberty University experienced
the presence of God in a revival that resulted in a fast for 60 hours.
The usual Wednesday night prayer meeting ended a little after 9:00
P.M., and the revival that transformed many lives began about
10:30 P.M.

The main auditorium of Thomas Road Baptist Church was
the students' main place to "hang out" because this infant university didn't have many facilities, and most students were living in
small houses around the church.

About 35 students were scattered in small groups throughout
the auditorium when a weeping young man stood behind the pulpit to announce, "You all think I'm saved, but I'm not. . . ." He con-

fessed his sins of lying, cheating on tests, being an egotist, and several other sins.

The shocked students listened intently until he went down to the pulpit stairs to pray. Some went to pray with him; others prayed for him in small groups. A reverential spirit gripped the room. Then over the sound of whispered prayers, another boy stood behind the pulpit. He, too, began, "You think I'm saved, but I've never received Christ. . . ." He too confessed his sins and went down the other side of the pulpit to pray. Several joined him.

Then the sound of the piano playing "Sweet Hour of Prayer" filled the prayer vacancies. A young lady had a key and had unlocked the piano cover and had begun playing. The background hymns didn't stop for approximately 60 hours. Other pianists sat on the front row waiting their turn to play. It's almost as if everyone agreed, "If the music stopped, the revival would end." Within a few minutes, melodious organ music joined the piano. There were also many willing organists to keep the revival going.

Next a girl gave the same testimony: "All of you think I'm saved because I was baptized as a young girl . . . but I'm not. . . ."

Around midnight, someone phoned Pastor Jerry Falwell and told him, "You'd better get down to church; revival's breaking out." He came in casual clothing without tie and suit. There was a sense of urgency. Throughout the night other students and church members felt a sudden urge to "come down to the church." Some received a phone call from friends; others were awakened by the Holy Spirit. By 6:00 A.M. more than 2,000 people filled the auditorium.

The university was shut down for two days; high-schoolers didn't go to school; those who owned businesses shut their doors. God's presence was in the church and no one wanted to leave. When students got so tired they couldn't stay awake, they slept under the pews; some even slept on the floor in the back foyer. When Jesus was there, who could leave? The crowd swelled to more than 4,000.

There was no formal preaching, but people formed a long line off to the left of the pulpit. When it came their time to speak, some confessed their sins; some announced that they had just prayed to receive Christ; others testified of their faith; others just requested a song to be sung by all or for some soloist to sing a favorite.

For 60 hours the mood of the audience swayed back and forth between reverential times of meditation to loud shouting of "Hallelujah!" or "AMEN."

The great revivals of Wheaton College and Asbury University were explosive. When the Holy Spirit came like a bombshell, people went everywhere spreading the revival spirit. The Liberty University revival was implosive. People were drawn into God's presence, and they dared not leave; they couldn't leave; they were like people being sucked into a whirlpool.

Many who had previously professed salvation were truly born again because they had only made an outward confession that wasn't of the heart. God showed many the hidden sin of their hearts. The proud had been boastful but now saw it as a sin of arrogance against God. Those who had many small sins that didn't hurt anyone repented when they realized their sin was against God. And of course there were some sensational testimonies of those who were hiding besetting sins.

Here's where the fasting comes in: Almost no one left the church to go out for a meal. Christ was the Bread of Life, and fellowshipping with Him satisfied any hunger that one may have had. People were so busy meeting with God that they didn't take the time to eat; no, they didn't want to eat.

One student who phoned out to have pizza delivered felt so guilty that most of the pizza ended up in the trash, even though there were multitudes who had not eaten for a day. Sometimes fasting becomes a struggle, but there are other times—like the revival at Liberty—when the Lord is so manifest that people forget about food: "Oh, taste and see that the LORD is good" (Ps. 34:8).

When God blessed the Liberty students with His presence, it was what I call the "atmospheric presence of God." Just as you can feel moisture on a cloudy day when there is no rain, so you can experience God's presence. Revival is defined when God pours out His presence on His people, as seen in the promise of the Lord: "I will pour out My Spirit on all flesh" (Joel 2:28).

In that 60-hour revival, God blessed the students of Liberty University because they fulfilled Scripture: "Blessed are those who hunger and thirst for righteousness, for they shall be filled" (Matt. 5:6).

The revival was broken about 7:00 P.M. on Saturday morning. A young man stood behind the pulpit to "confess" his sins. He included some sexual conduct in high school, but it seemed more like bragging. People didn't sense a sorrow for sin, nor was there brokenness. It's as though the Holy Spirit said, "I'll have no part of this," and He removed His presence.

Many students left for Christian service assignments, and the leader struggled to keep the meeting going. But around 9:00 A.M., everyone realized it was over; so a benediction was prayed and everyone went home.[1]

Now What?

This revival was about the Holy Spirit showing people their sin when they sought God's face and fasted and repented of their sin. You are now in a 10- or 21-day Daniel Fast, praying for a particular project or for a reason that God has put upon your heart. What does this event say to you?

Perhaps God led you into this 10- or 21-day Daniel Fast to show you some sin of attitude, actions or contemplation. Perhaps God wants you to deal with a sin before He gives you the big breakout you seek.

Let's look at reasons why there may be a barrier to your spiritual victory. Sin could be a small, insidious thing that's hindering your spiritual progress, but you might not be aware of it. Why?

Sometimes we're blinded to our sin. It's there, but we don't see it. We're like a man with cancer who has a hidden growth in his colon that's sapping his strength, but he doesn't know it. He used to walk 18 holes of golf and carry his clubs. But slowly he lost his strength, so he rode in a cart. Then he cut the game to 9 holes because he got so tired. Finally, cancer cut his stamina so he didn't even want to play. Then a colonoscopy revealed cancer; he had an operation and now he's back to 18 holes of golf.

Sin—like cancer—cuts into our spiritual strength so we can't do the things for God we used to do. Then sin kills our stamina. We don't want to pray or read our Bibles or even go to church where we praise and worship God.

Before sins binds up our strength, it blinds us. "Satan, the god of this evil world, has blinded the minds of those who don't believe, so they are unable to see the glorious light of the Good News that is shining upon them. They don't understand the message we preach about the glory of Christ, who is the exact likeness of God" (2 Cor. 4:4, *NLT*).

The longer you remain in the light, the more you realize what God is trying to tell you. In the Daniel Fast, God begins to show you the hidden sins that block the flow of His blessings. Like trash in the fuel line, the engine is poking along with half power. When you get rid of the trash, the flow of energy-producing gasoline will give new life to the engine.

But just knowing about your hidden sin is not enough. You must confess it to God to get forgiveness. "If we confess our sins, He is faithful and just to forgive our sins and cleanse us" (1 John 1:9).

Remember, confession means more than just recognition of its presence in your life. When you *confess*, you say the same thing about your sin that God says. When God says it's hideous, you must agree with Him and put it out of your sight.

Take cursing for an illustration. Some Christians treat cursing as a bad habit; or they excuse it with a bad temper or an emotional outbreak. But note what God thinks: "The LORD will not hold him guiltless who takes His name in vain" (Exod. 20:7).

When you fast for a long time, you begin to see things as God sees them. When you see how terrible your sin is, you don't have to "make" yourself repent. You don't have to make yourself give up a sin that's hard to give up. Fasting in God's presence gives you strength, and you say, "I can do all things through Christ who strengthens me" (Phil. 4:13).

My Time to Pray

Lord, I seek Your presence in my life. You have said, "You will seek Me and find Me, when you search for Me with all your heart" (Jer. 29:13).

Lord, I yield my whole life to You, including my mind, my attitude and the things I like to do. I take my control off these things.

Lord, fill me with Your Holy Spirit to study Your Word, to pray and to serve You.

Lord, take away my blindness and show me any sin that blocks Your blessing in my life.

Lord, I confess my sin (by name), and I ask You to forgive me and cleanse me. Amen.

My Answers Today

_____

_____

_____

_____

_____

_____

_____

_____

_____

_____

_____

Note
1. Elmer Towns, *What's Right with the Church* (Ventura, CA: Regal Books, 2009), pp. 84-86. See also Elmer Towns, *The Ten Greatest Revivals Ever* (Ann Arbor, MI: Servant Publications, 2000), pp. 13-14.

For suggested recipes, see pages 180-192.

❧ DAY 14 ❧

Don't Violate Your Fast

One obvious value of fasting lies in the fact that its discipline helps us keep the body in its place. It is a practical acknowledgment of the supremacy of the spiritual. But in addition to this relaxing value, fasting has direct benefits in relation to prayer as well. Many who practice it from right motives and in order to give themselves more unreservedly to prayer testify that the mind becomes unusually clear and vigorous. There are a noticeable spiritual quickening and increased power of concentration on the things of the Spirit.

J. OSWALD SANDERS

What happens when you slip and eat—when you eat something that you vowed that you wouldn't eat? That's a tough question. Tough, because the slip is against God; you violated your promise to God. Tough, because the slip is also against yourself; you promised yourself to pray and fast.

Let's start with an unintentional violation of your fast. You ask how eating something can be unintentional. Isn't eating a choice? Not always.

I walked out to the receptionist in the School of Religion where my office is located. It was the Halloween season and the receptionist had a dish of "friendly" candy corn on her desk. It was her way of saying hello to those who come to Liberty University's School of Religion.

I began talking to her about a project and without thinking I popped a couple of candy corn pieces into my mouth and began chewing them. Before I could swallow, the impact of food—just a little—in my mouth dawned on me.

DEFINITIONS

To violate a fast is to breach the limits of your diet or the length of your vow that you made to God.

To break a fast is to come to the completion of the time and commitment of the fast and begin eating a normal diet.

"Ohh!" I smacked my forehead, realizing what a foolish act I had just committed.

"Ohh . . ." I continued to moan as though I had cut my finger with a knife or slammed a car door on my finger. I was thinking of the fingers holding more candy corn, like the original candy corn that committed the infraction.

"Ohh . . ." I agonized when I realized I'd just lost three days of a 10-day fast. Three days lost, and I'd have to begin again for another whole 10 days. I couldn't just say "whoops!" and keep going.

What do you do if you unintentionally violate your Daniel Fast? That's easy to answer. You do what I did. First, I immediately prayed and asked God to forgive my "ignorant" sin. That's when you are not aware of what you are doing. You presumably are innocent because you didn't know what you were doing. But try telling that to the cop who pulled you over for speeding 60 miles per hour in a 35-mile-per-hour speed zone.

In the Old Testament there was a severe penalty for presumptuous sin (intentionally sinning) and less penalty for sins of ignorance (not realizing you were breaking God's law; see Num. 15:29-31). So what do you do if you ignorantly violate your Daniel Fast, like I did? First I began eating a regular meal because I had violated my fast. Second, I asked God to forgive me of an ignorant sin. "If we confess our sins, He . . . forgives" (1 John 1:9). Third, I asked God to keep me from doing it again, "Keep me from hidden faults" (Ps. 19:12, *ELT*).

Since the reason for my fast had not been accomplished, I waited some time and began my 10-day fast a second time.

I'd like to tell you that God answered my prayer and I never ignorantly broke my fast again. But the second time was just as ignorant as the first. It was the Valentine season and I walked out to the same receptionist again with a task for her to do. This time she had chocolate kisses wrapped in silver paper. Whereas the first time I "popped" candy corn into my mouth without any effort, this time I had to unwrap the silver paper, all the time not realizing what I was doing until I was chewing chocolate.

"Should I spit it out?" I quickly asked. But realizing what had happened, I swallowed the rest of the candy kiss. I stopped my fast; I didn't begin again for another week. I followed the same procedure as before.

The Daniel Fast is a partial fast, so you are eating something. It should be easy to discipline your food intake concerning certain items. But suppose you violate your fast because you give in to temptation. The Bible calls that a presumptuous sin, and instructs you to pray, "Keep back your servant from presumptuous sins" (Ps. 19:13).

There are several layers to this problem. First, you scandalized will. You have hurt your willpower by doing the thing you vowed not to do. This impacts your self-perception and weakens your self-esteem. By violating your vow, you might build a negative self-image. This is the person who hates himself and perhaps violates his conscience to punish himself.

So how do you soothe your self-esteem and begin again to build self-discipline? You can't do it in yourself. Even Paul said, "The evil I will not to do, that I practice" (Rom. 7:19). Paul was frustrated because of this: "For what I am doing, I do not understand" (Rom. 7:15).

The answer to Paul's broken vows and unfulfilled commitments was the Lord. "I thank God—through Jesus Christ our Lord" (Rom. 7:25). You need the power of Christ to help you.

If you've violated your vow, remember that it's not just against yourself and your standards; you have sinned against God. "When you make a vow to God, do not delay to pay it" (Eccles. 5:4). Why? Because "Your mouth is making you sin" (Eccles. 5:6, *TLB*).

Don't try to fool God by saying you didn't understand how hard a Daniel Fast would be, or you didn't really understand when you made a vow. "Don't try to defend yourself by telling . . . that it was all a mistake [to make the vow]. That would make God very angry" (Eccles. 5:6, *TLB*).

Only in your private audience with God will you understand how serious it is to break your vow to God. When you pray privately, your words will choke you. When you pray out loud, the ceiling will turn to lead and your prayers will bounce back to you. Your heart will condemn you and you will realize you can't pray for the spiritual good for which you intended to fast.

But you've also let others down. If you formed a prayer bond by "agreeing" with them, will God answer them because you've broken the circle of agreement? Only you can determine that answer as you wait before God.

The depths of your conviction will determine the depth of your confession. You should cry out to be restored to God's presence, "Why do You hide Your face from me?" (Ps. 88:14). You haven't lost your relationship with God; you've only lost your fellowship with Him. Again David prayed, "Sometimes I ask God . . . why am I walking around in tears, harassed by enemies" (Ps. 42:9, *THE MESSAGE*).

Don't get down on yourself, because "The blood of Jesus Christ His Son cleanses us from all sin" (1 John 1:7). The word "all" means that God forgives deep sins like murder and theft, but He also forgives things like broken promises.

Then realize that God deals with you in mercy, just as He dealt with Paul who confessed his many sins but recognized, "God had mercy on me" (1 Tim. 1:13, *TLB*).

Then begin your Daniel Fast again, not where you left off. Begin again from the beginning, whether it's for 3 days, 10 days or 21 days. Enter the Daniel Fast with joy because you were forgiven all past violation. Begin again with all the faith that you exercised the first time.

My Time to Pray

Lord, I enter a Daniel Fast with all my integrity, and I will keep it to the end.

Lord, if I ignorantly violate my fast, forgive me for my unintended mistake.

Lord, if I presumptuously violate my Daniel Fast, forgive me and strengthen my will. I will begin again to keep the original vow I made to You.

Lord, deal with me in mercy, and give me strength to pray and fast; hear the intercessions of my heart for the spiritual goal I've set. Amen.

My Answers Today

_____

_____

_____

_____

_____

_____

_____

_____

_____

_____

_____

_____

_____

_____

_____

_____

For suggested recipes, see pages 180-192.

Days 15 to Day 21 Overview

Learn About Specific Prayers

In the final week of your fast, you'll learn how to receive the crucifixion of Jesus into your prayer life (Day 15) and you'll learn the role of weeping when you fast and pray (Day 16).

You have been fasting for at least two weeks, so you've spent some extra time in God's presence. Day 17 will tell you the strengths of introspective prayers and, most importantly, how to come out of the desert of introspection or discouragement and pray for your faith goal. Also, you need to be reminded that there is a time to rest in prayer (Day 18).

Then you'll read about urgent prayers (Day 19) and warfare prayers (Day 20). Because Satan is your enemy, be vigilant in prayer.

The last day's reading will challenge you to stay in each moment and pray to the end of your fast.

Daily Readings

Day 15: The Prayer of Crucifixion
Day 16: Weeping While Praying
Day 17: Introspective Prayer
Day 18: Resting in Prayer
Day 19: Urgent Prayer
Day 20: Spiritual Warfare Prayer
Day 21: Stay in the Moment

❧ DAY 15 ❧

The Prayer of Crucifixion

*As a Boomer, I have been conditioned to enjoy the best the world has
to offer. Fasting speaks boldly to consumerism, one of my generational core
values. To set aside what I want so that I encourage personal spiritual growth
is what it means to deny myself and take up my cross daily in this present age.
I suspect it would be difficult for me to rise to the challenge
of discipleship and live a consistently Christian lifestyle without
practicing the discipline of fasting.*

DOUGLAS PORTER

During your Daniel Fast, you will be tempted to quit in many different ways; most of the temptations will be very subtle, so that you may not even recognize them as temptations. Whether temptations are subtle or blatant calls to gross immorality, you must successfully face them and triumph over them.

Perhaps fasting is something you've never done, so be careful. Satan may probably not tempt you to overt outward sin, but he may tempt you to do less, like tempting you to quit fasting before you reach the conclusion. You may be tempted to eat just a little "bite" of the thing you promised to give up for Christ. Or, Satan may tempt you to end your fast one or two days early.

I was saved on July 25, 1950, and six weeks later I went off to Bible College. Satan couldn't trip me up with outward sin, so he pushed me to excesses, i.e., to being fanatical.

I was greatly motivated by a sermon on self-crucifixion in chapel that was preached from Romans: "Knowing this, that our old man is crucified with him, that the body of sin might be destroyed, that henceforth we should not serve sin" (Rom. 6:6, *KJV*). The speaker emphasized "is crucified," which told us it was something we students must do.

Next, the speaker challenged us from Galatians: "And those who are Christ's have crucified the flesh with its passions and desires" (Gal. 5:24). He asked, "What have you crucified today?"

Nothing, I thought. So I decided to find something to crucify. I decided to give up Ping-Pong—something I liked doing—for a week. Then I quickly added, *No softball with the guys.* That was hard, but I did it!

All the men's dorms were heated from a central furnace, and all the heat was turned off around 9:00 P.M. each evening. The room was getting colder as I began praying around 10:30 P.M. I only wore underwear to sleep in, so I began to shiver as I continued kneeling by my bed. I was tempted to jump under a warm blanket but rationalized, *No . . . I crucified my desire for physical warmth.*

I felt that praying in the cold was a way to "crucify the flesh with its affections and lusts." I kept telling myself, *If you love Jesus, you'll crucify the flesh and keep praying in the cold.* After 10 or 15 minutes, I was shivering so hard I couldn't keep my mind on my request; I was struggling inwardly against jumping into the bed. I couldn't pray out loud to focus my thoughts because my jaw shivered too much.

Finally, I rationalized, *God looks at my heart; He doesn't pay attention to my body.* I jumped under the covers, but not to go to sleep. I hunkered down on my hands and head on the bed, with my knees pulled under my body. I went back to praying. I justified myself by saying that prayer came easier as I enjoyed the warmth of the protective blanket.

Then guilt set in. I began to rationalize, *If you really love Jesus, you'd suffer the cold as you pray.* So, to "crucify" any selfish urges for warmth, I got out from under the blanket and knelt in the cold. For two or three minutes, I "felt" victorious over temptation. I felt

I was "crucifying" the bodily urge for warmth. So I prayed with ease when I was only chilly.

After about five to seven minutes, I really got cold and my jaw started shaking again. I couldn't keep my thoughts on what I was praying. Finally, I concluded, *This is stupid,* so I hunkered down again under the covers and began praying. As I got warmer, prayer got easier. Then after five to seven minutes, guilt again set in and I rationalized, *If you love Jesus, you'd pray in the cold.* I thought of how much Jesus suffered for me in His crucifixion. So again I decided to "crucify" myself.

You would have laughed if you had been in that dark dorm room to see me get in and out of bed several times. As a matter of fact, I think God probably laughed at the naïve freshman who was filled with both love and guilt, trying to demonstrate something by jumping in and out of bed.

The problem is that the chapel speaker wrongly applied the idea of crucifixion. Jesus did it all and cried, "It is finished!" (John 19:30). My crucifixion of my flesh can't add anything to Jesus' crucifixion. My crucifixion was just plain old works. The Bible teaches, "Not of works, lest anyone should boast" (Eph. 2:9).

I didn't understand that "crucifixion" is something I *receive* from God, not something I *do* for God. I think the chapel speaker had wrongly applied crucifixion because the old *King James* translates it, "Our old man *is* crucified" (Rom. 6:6, *KJV*, emphasis added), suggesting a present tense verb action. But look carefully at the *New King James Version*: "Our old man was crucified with Him." The verb "crucified" is past action in the original language.

Our crucifixion is a past action; our old nature was crucified when Christ died. We are not to *do* it, but *receive* it. Paul explains it as follows: "I have been crucified [past tense] with Christ" (Gal. 2:20). Christ was crucified in the past, and Paul identified with the cross in his life that he lived after the crucifixion.

When Jesus died, He died all the way. No life was left. When we try to "crucify" ourselves (like praying when it's too cold), we don't die all the way. The old sin nature will tempt us as long as there's life left in this body. However, when we properly "crucify" ourselves, we receive what Christ has done and we apply His death to our sin. Paul said, "I through the law died to the law that I might live to God" (Gal. 2:19). That means we yield ourselves to God and receive His life to triumph over temptation and sin.

This type of life is more about completely yielding ourselves (the inner person) to God rather than doing something to get victory. It's not about us being victorious but Christ being victorious through us. Some call this the "crucified life," while others call it the "transformed life" or the "victorious life." Some refer to it as the "exchanged life"; i.e., "I was in Christ when He died, and now I yield for Him to come into my life."

Paul told us how this exchanged life takes place: "God forbid that I should boast except in the cross of our Lord Jesus Christ, by whom the world has been crucified to me, and I to the world" (Gal. 6:14). When we are "crucified" to the world, we take up all that the cross symbolizes. It means humiliation, degradation and an end to sin. So when we take up the cross, we yield ourselves to God and determine to sin no more.

That doesn't mean we lose our sin nature. No, we still have an old nature that will tempt us to sin (see 1 John 1:8). But we surrender ourselves to God to get His victory over it. Nor does it mean that we will never sin again. We will sin, for John teaches that the one who thinks he has stopped sinning is deceived: "If we say that we have not sinned, we make Him a liar, and His word is not in us" (1 John 1:10). What it does mean is that when we "crucify" ourselves—or take up our cross—we also take on the victory of Christ who triumphed over sin in His death. His death gave us life, so we get the energy of Christ's life when we receive His crucifixion.

Dying to Self-Effort

Jesus challenged, "If anyone desires to come after Me, let him deny himself, and take up his cross daily, and follow Me" (Luke 9:23). That doesn't mean we carry a large, heavy cross, as some have done. It doesn't mean we wear a cross as jewelry, or even erect a cross in front of our home.

Jesus was describing our death to self-effort and earthly desire. Jesus continued this thought in the next verse: "For whoever desires to save his life will lose it, but whoever loses his life for My sake will save it" (Luke 9:24). To lose your life is to do only the will of Christ, not your own selfish will. We lose our life by giving up our earthly desires in order to pursue what Jesus deserves.

Notice the next verse, which tells us we gain nothing by pursuing our desires: "What profit is it to a man if he gains the whole world, and is himself destroyed or lost?" (Luke 9:25). Everything the world has to offer will not compare to the inner life that Jesus gives.

According to Jesus, the issue is that we quit (we yield) thinking what the world cares about or what the world has or what the world promises. In the next verse Jesus says, "For whoever is ashamed of Me and My words, of him the Son of Man will be ashamed when He comes in His own glory" (Luke 9:26).

Crucifying yourself does not mean doing something "religious" or following "good works" to prove yourself to God. You completely surrender yourself to God, allowing Jesus to act within you, by allowing His life to be your energy or power over sin.

Not Physical Death, but Our Inward Death

There are a group of men in the Philippines who allow themselves to be nailed to a cross each year on Good Friday. That's because Jesus died on Good Friday. Wealthy tourists, journalists and a large crowd watch these Filipino men attempt to identify with Christ by being nailed to a cross. One man, a commercial sign maker in his forties, has gone through this "penitence" ritual 21 times.[1]

Self-crucifixion is one of the most abused phenomena of Christianity. Those who do it misinterpret Paul's statement, "And those who are Christ's have crucified the flesh with its passions and desires" (Gal. 5:24). As a result, monks have starved themselves, prayed in snow, beaten themselves with whips (as Christ was beaten), gnashed themselves, placed crude crowns of thorns on their heads, and done all forms of torture. Others have lived in isolation; still others have gone without talking for seven years or longer. Still others have refused marriage, or any of the other good gifts God has given to us (see Jas. 1:17).

God did not intend any of these things when He asked us to become crucified with Christ. We simply receive what Christ has done for us in His crucifixion. We receive His death for the forgiveness of sins; we receive His life for the power to live above our selfish desires. His life gives us strength to overcome temptation.

The problem is that we like to make ourselves look good because we suffer when people criticize us or laugh at us or reject us. So we go through life trying to make ourselves look good, or we play a role. We usually play several roles to make us appealing to the different groups of people we live around.

When we "crucify" ourselves, we yield to Christ so that what He thinks of us matters more than what others think of us. We no longer live to look good to others. Oh yes, we are good neighbors and good testimonies; and we don't want to do stupid things or look weird. But we quit the hypocrite's role to make people think we are something we're not.

So to crucify yourself, you please God first, family second and others third. We live for a new purpose, one suggested by John the Baptist: "He must increase, but I must decrease" (John 3:30).

When we crucify ourselves, we live by a new value system. We give up our inner compulsions for self-power, self-protection, self-success, and gathering "stuff." We give everything to God for His control, and we use what He lets us use.

We no longer have to "win" for selfish reasons. We learn that losing everything to God is much more satisfying than winning the world. For when we lose to God, we win the most important thing in life—being in the center of God's will.

No one likes the idea of dying. All normal people struggle to stay alive. But what if you were to die today? Would life go on without you? Yes! Did life get along fairly well before you were born? Yes! So our life is not necessarily needed.

However, when we die to self, we live to God. When we die, we become important to God, and He uses us. When we die to self, we become necessary to God.

To crucify our self is another way of dealing with our pride. In the act of yielding completely to God, we become more humble. Didn't James tell us, "Humble yourselves in the sight of the Lord, and He will lift you up" (Jas. 4:10)? So our humility is important to God if He's going to use us.

Humility is an interesting word. *Webster* says it means, "to reduce oneself to the lowest position in one's own eyes, and, or the eyes of another."[2] It comes from the word *humus*, which means "from the earth." Humus is that rich organic soil that is formed from the partial decomposition of plant or animal matter. Look deeply: the rich soil that produces new life comes from the death of other matter. So when you "crucify" yourself—or you die—you produce an experience that gives new life from God.

Doesn't our life represent a seed that can be planted by God to give life to others? Remember, Jesus said, "Except a seed is planted in the ground and dies, it abides alone: but if it dies, it brings forth much fruit" (John 12:24, *ELT*). So when we crucify ourselves, others prosper and live.

So our life must be open to the renewing rain and the richness of the soil and the energy of the sun to produce new life in us and others. But that new life is brought forth with *humus,* or the death of self.

Trying to become humble is like trying to go to sleep. The harder you try, the more difficult it becomes. But when we surrender to sleep, like surrendering to the Lord, what we seek will happen. You can't deliberately pray for humility, nor can you work it up; it's a gift from God.

Fasting and Self-Crucifixion

You are on a Daniel Fast that will last 10 or 21 days. Don't be deceived. You will not become more spiritual just because you fast. Refraining from food will not get you any merit before God. Fasting is a discipline whereby you control your body to give more attention to God. When you fast, you meditate more on God, and you pray more often and more deeply. Fasting is simply a means to the end; the result is that you form a deeper relationship with God. It is God who gives the results you seek.

Fasting may drive another nail in the cross of self-crucifixion, but it doesn't make you more holy or a better prayer intercessor. And there are other acts of self-crucifixion that are effective, such as breaking up with a steady who doesn't know Christ, or when you turn down a job because it would compromise your faith, or when you sacrifice some of your money you were saving for a luxury item to give it to the cause of Christ. There are acts of self-crucifixion—when properly yielded—that will cause you to grow in Christ.

Most likely, self-crucifixion comes in small, intentional acts when we give part of our life to God. Doing without food will not gain you merit, but when you put Christ first to intercede for a prayer project instead of eating, that will be honored by Christ.

Small, unrecognizable victories over self-pleasure or self-promotion or satisfying your lust will often not be seen by others, but they will lead to the greatest amount of spiritual growth in our lives.

My Time to Pray

Lord, I acknowledge that I have a big "ego." Please teach me to put Christ first in all I do. Teach me humility.

Lord, I can't crucify myself by anything I pray or do; I receive the benefit of Christ's death to forgive my sin.

Lord, I can't become more spiritual by spending more time in prayer. I receive the life of Jesus that comes from His triumph over death. I yield to Christ and will be strong against temptation in His indwelling presence.

Lord, I will give up little things that hinder my spiritual life and big lusts that would destroy my life. I claim Your victory over temptation. I want to grow in continual steps that bring me closer to You. Amen.

My Answers Today

_____
_____
_____
_____
_____
_____
_____
_____
_____
_____
_____
_____
_____
_____

Notes
1. See http://www.msnbc.msn.com/id/17978154/ (accessed June 4, 2009).
2. *Webster's Dictionary, 11th edition,* s.v. "humble."

For suggested recipes, see pages 180-192.

❧ DAY 16 ❧

Weeping While Praying

"Now, therefore," says the Lord, "Turn to Me with all your heart,
With fasting, with weeping, and with mourning."

JOEL 2:12

Have you ever prayed so hard that you began to weep? Maybe when you got saved you were so convicted of your sin that you wept before God. Today, let's talk about weeping as you pray. Will tears help your prayers get answered?

The Bible teaches that there is "A time to weep, And a time to laugh" (Eccles. 3:4). So when should we weep with our prayers? Also, is there a time to laugh when we pray?

If our eyes are always dry, it probably means our soul is also dry. Because, like the sun that bakes the clay, something could have hardened our heart.

On the other hand, when we shed tears before God, it probably means God has touched the very center of our feelings. He has scratched away the scab that has protected a raw wound that needs healing. God can probably scratch away a hardened scab that even we ourselves couldn't remove.

Many people weep when they first come to Jesus. A woman who was broken over her sin came and stood behind Jesus as He ate at a banquet in Simon the Pharisee's house. "[She] stood at His feet behind Him weeping; and she began to wash His feet with her tears, and wiped them with the hair of her head; and she kissed His feet and anointed them with the fragrant oil" (Luke 7:38).

Simon criticized the woman, probably for her tears, and probably for creating a scene in his house. But mostly Simon criticized
Jesus, thinking to himself, "This man, if He were a prophet, would
know who and what manner of woman this is who is touching
Him" (Luke 7:39). Jesus knew Simon's thoughts and told him a
story about canceled debt; and then He defended the woman, saying, " 'Therefore I say to you, her sins, which are many, are forgiven,
for she loved much. But to whom little is forgiven, the same loves
little.' Then He said to her, 'Your sins are forgiven' " (Luke 7:47-48).
There's nothing wrong with weeping our way to the cross for salvation. But not all people shed tears when they are saved.

In 1957, I pastored a church in West Dallas where many Mexican-
Americans lived. We had prayed long for the mother of the Rodriquez
family to get saved. Her three boys and husband were already converted. Mrs. Rodriquez was deeply touched at our Communion service and raised her hand to be saved at the end of the service. As she
was led to Christ, she laughed uncontrollably; she laughed so much
that I was asked to come help out with the situation.

Mrs. Rodriquez told of climbing steps at a Catholic cathedral in
Mexico to get forgiveness, but nothing happened. She had wept at
many liturgical services, but her sins weren't forgiven. When she
learned there was nothing she could do to obtain salvation but believe in Jesus, a great burden was rolled off her back. All she had to
do was invite Jesus into her heart. Hearing about grace, she began to
laugh with the joy of freedom in Christ.

Were you saved with tears or laughter? Even after salvation,
weeping can become a part of prayer. Sometimes we weep over sin in
our life. Sometimes tears are natural because of our failures or dis-
appointments, or when circumstances turn against us. We weep over
the death of someone close to us, even if it was his or her time to die.

When Mary's brother Lazarus died, "Jesus saw her weeping"
(John 11:33). It's only natural to cry when a part of your life is taken
away in death. It's both you and the other person who has lost
something to death. Jesus also wept (see John 11:35), not only for
Lazarus but also for the unbelief of Mary, Martha, His disciples and
the Jews. He wept because they rejected Him; no one thought He

could conquer death. Don't you feel like crying sometimes when you're rejected?

Perhaps you're praying for a Daniel Fast project, and if your prayers are not answered, it will result in a financial loss, a spiritual defeat or a loss in the eyes of those who knew you were fasting, and also a loss of your spiritual vow to God. When we suffer loss, our hearts should break like a dam where stored-up waters begin to flow.

Sometimes our memory causes us to weep. The Jews who were taken captive to Babylon remembered the good times in the Promised Land and the presence of God in the Temple. Their sin led to God's punishment, and Babylon took them into captivity. They cried, "By the rivers of Babylon, there we sat down, yea, we wept when we remembered Zion" (Ps. 137:1). Their captors asked them to sing their psalms. They answered, "How shall we sing the LORD's song in a foreign land?" (Ps. 137:4). There is a time to put away enjoyment and weep over the memory of what we have lost.

Sometimes you will weep over lost loved ones. Perhaps you have added to your fast prayer for the salvation of lost people who are special to you. Paul felt that way when he prayed for lost Jews: "I have great sorrow and continual grief in my heart. For I could wish that I myself were accursed from Christ for my brethren, my countrymen according to the flesh" (Rom. 9:2-3). His tears were not for what he lost, but for those who were lost. Sometimes you will weep over sins in your life, and probably the greater the sin, the greater the tears.

King David committed adultery with Bathsheba, and, to cover up his sin, he had her husband killed. Are there greater sins than adultery and murder? What makes these sins so terrible? "But the thing that David had done displeased the LORD" (2 Sam. 11:27). Every sin is against God, but when we come to realize our sin has personally hurt God, it's then that we weep.

> David therefore pleaded with God for the child, and David fasted and went in and lay all night on the ground. So the elders of his house arose and went to him, to raise him up

from the ground. But he would not, nor did he eat food with them (2 Sam. 12:16-17).

Out of his deep repentance, David wrote Psalm 51, which reflected his deep repentance with tears before God.

> For I acknowledge my transgressions, And my sin is always before me (Ps. 51:3).

> Against You, You only, have I sinned, and done this evil in Your sight. . . . Hide Your face from my sins, And blot out all my iniquities (Ps. 51:4,9).

It's much easier to search for your sin when you deal with it in a biblical way. If you harden your heart and act as if you have no sin, God will eventually break your heart and He will deal harshly with your sin. If you know anything about God, He'll be more severe on your sin than you will be. So deal with it yourself and save yourself some added pain.

Also, be careful about praying for God to break your heart. He may do it and cause you more pain than if you dealt with the sin immediately and completely.

When God breaks your heart, it may be as severe as when you lost a loved one that you thought you couldn't lose. There may have been a time in the past when the pain was so severe that you thought you couldn't go on living. If God has to break your heart, you may have to go through that pain again, only it will be more severe.

How do you deal with known sin? First, recognize disobedience in your life and call it what God calls it—sin. Don't blame your sin nature that tempts you to sin: "If we say that we have no sin, we deceive ourselves, and the truth is not in us" (1 John 1:8). Also, don't say you never even sinned one time: "If we say that we have not sinned, we make Him a liar, and His word is not in us" (1 John 1:10).

Second, confess your sin to God, which means you recognize your sin for what it is: "If we confess our sins, He is faithful and just to forgive us our sins and to cleanse us from all unrighteousness" (1 John 1:9). Did you notice that God cleanses *after* we confess it to Him?

Next, realize that God forgives all sin, with an emphasis on *all*. "If we walk in the light as He is in the light, we have fellowship with one another, and the blood of Jesus Christ His Son cleanses us from *all* sin" (1 John 1:7, emphasis added).

Fourth, you must forsake your sin and then determine not to do it again. Fast and pray: "And do not lead us into temptation" (Matt. 6:13).

Finally, learn a lesson from the experience so you will be stronger and can live above that particular temptation.

My Time to Pray

Lord, show me the sin that hinders my prayer life;
I'll confess and repent.

Lord, I repent and turn from sin that blocks my
fellowship with You.

Lord, Your forgiveness feels good; I enjoy praying
in Your presence. Amen.

My Answers Today

_____

_____

_____

_____

_____

_____

_____

_____

_____

For suggested recipes, see pages 180-192.

❧ DAY 17 ❧

Introspective Prayer

*Even if we wanted to, we could not manipulate God. We fast and pray
for results, but the results are in God's hands. One of the greatest spiritual
benefits of fasting is becoming more attentive to God—becoming more
aware of our own inadequacies and His adequacy, our own contingencies
and His self-sufficiency—and listening to what He wants us to be and do.
Christian fasting, therefore, is totally antithetical to, say, Hindu fasting.
Both seek results; however, Hindu fasting focuses on the self and tries to get
something for a perceived sacrifice. Christian fasting focuses on God.
The results are spiritual results that glorify God—both in the person who
fasts and others for whom we fast and pray.*

ELMER L. TOWNS

Have you ever felt like you were wandering in a desert and you
didn't know which way to go? The horizon seemed distant, and
nothing was familiar. Have you ever felt lost and didn't know
which way to turn?

The psalmist also felt lost: "In the day of my trouble I sought
the Lord . . . my soul refused to be comforted" (Ps. 77:2). Again he
cried, "As for me, my feet had almost stumbled; My steps had
nearly slipped" (Ps. 73:2).

And complained: "Do not hide Your face from me in the day
of my trouble" (Ps. 102:2). The psalmist felt lost and couldn't find
God. Have you ever felt like the ceiling of your room was made of
iron, and your prayers bounced back in your face? When you cried
out to God, did it seem like He wasn't there?

When that happens, most people retreat into introspective prayer. Fasting can be a dark time in their life and they feel hopeless and helpless. All this leads to depression. They feel they can't begin to fast and pray for a prayer project.

Some people complain to God or they complain about God. Instead of reaching up to God or reaching out to others, they retreat inward. They blame themselves, and as a result, they feel even more hopeless and helpless.

Job's prayers are perhaps the best example in the Bible of introspective prayers. He did nothing wrong; there was no outward sin in his life that he should be judged by God. Yet most people know well that he was the victim of violence, family loss, theft and bankruptcy. Job went through incredible suffering and pain, yet he was godly; and no one could accuse him of transgressions. Job was blameless.

Job's cattle were stolen by raiders; his sheep and employees were killed; lightning burned up his crops; and a tornado or hurricane collapsed a house on his children, killing them all. In a different raid upon his possessions, more camels were stolen and more servants were murdered (see Job 1:13-19).

The day we all dread financially came to Job, yet "he fell to the ground and worshiped" (Job 1:20). Instead of complaining, Job exercised faith in God: "Naked I came from my mother's womb, and naked shall I return there. The LORD gave, and the LORD has taken away; blessed be the name of the LORD" (Job 1:21).

Satan, who had masterminded the first wave of persecution, then attacked Job personally. Job developed terribly painful boils that hurt him so severely that he sat in ashes to dry the mucous and scraped himself with the sharp edges of broken pottery shards to relieve his suffering.

That is the day we all dread physically. Job agreed. "For the thing I greatly feared has come upon me, and what I dreaded has happened to me" (Job 3:25). Introspective prayer is always rooted in fear.

When we can't deal with fear, we end up in hopelessness. We give up like Job seemed to give up. "My days are swifter than a weaver's shuttle, and are spent without hope. Oh, remember that my life is a breath! My eye will never again see good" (Job 7:6-7).

His wife also gave up. She was no support to him in his suffering. She told Job, "Do you still hold fast to your integrity? Curse God and die!" (Job 2:9).

There may be times in your life when you feel abandoned by God. Maybe the prayer project for which you are fasting has you discouraged. Maybe you're doubting that God will answer, and you're about to give up.

Yet the Bible is filled with promises that God will come to us when we completely throw ourselves on His mercy and beg for His presence. "This poor man cried out, and the LORD heard him, and saved him out of all his troubles" (Ps. 34:6).

Then later the psalmist promised, "The LORD is near to those who have a broken heart, and saves such as have a contrite spirit . . . but the LORD delivers him out of them all" (Ps. 34:18-19).

Sometimes it's not sin that has us stranded in the desert. Maybe we've taken a wrong turn on the pathway. We've made the wrong decision and miss God's will. So we didn't commit a sin of rebellion or deliberate transgression. Maybe we ignored God's instructions, or we didn't seek His plan for our life. Maybe that's why the One in heaven is silent.

The Lord sometimes allows us to wander off the straight and narrow way because we need to learn the lesson, "Not My will, but Yours, be done" (Luke 22:42).

Maybe God didn't yell at us to call us back to the straight and narrow because we weren't listening to Him. We probably wouldn't have obeyed if He did yell. When we don't pay attention to the biblical signposts, or the inward Holy Spirit, would we have heeded His yell?

Sometimes we get lost in the desert because we were inattentive. Maybe God was trying to direct our lives, but we were too busy with our own business to do His will. So God let us get lost so we will feel the consequences of a life without God's presence. Then we get scared and begin our own yelling.

When I was five years old, Mother took me to downtown Savannah, Georgia, for Christmas shopping. She had a large multicolored tapestry handbag and told me to hang on to the strap.

Everywhere she went shopping, I hung on to the strap as we min-gled in the crowd. I remember it was in Woolworth's five-and-dime store that I let go of the bag to examine a pearl-handled six-shooter I wanted for Christmas.

Then I saw the tapestry bag leave, so I ran to grab the strap. As we were crossing Broughton Street, an elderly African-American lady looked down at me and asked, "Why are you holding on to my bag?"

I let out a blood-curdling scream that attracted a policeman who lifted me into his arms and held me till my mother arrived.

I didn't get lost because I wanted to leave Mother. I just didn't pay attention to what was necessary. Is that you? Now, if you spend time fasting in God's presence, you may find your way back to where you got lost.

When God talks to us and we don't listen, what does He do? He can yell—He can also shout—but usually does something dif-ferent. God does the opposite; He stops talking. He's silent until we're ready to listen to Him. By seemingly abandoning us for a while, God gets our attention and we desperately search for Him.

There's one great thing we learn from being lost in the desert—we learn self-knowledge. One of the best lessons we can learn in life is what we can't do in life. It's even a better gift than learning what we can do.

Remember, there are only a few things that most of us can do best, and then a few more things we do tolerably well; but there are hundreds of thousands of things we can't do. Blessed is the one who knows the boundaries of his spiritual abilities!

The foundation of self-knowledge is the basis upon which you build the rest of your life. When you know yourself well, you can make additions, subtractions and changes. You build a well-rounded spirituality when you build on a proper understanding of yourself.

However, if you spend the rest of your life in introspective prayer, you'll have a miserable, empty life. You won't just feel de-feated; you'll be defeated. Temptations will easily trip you and sin will blind you to the perfect will of God.

How does a blind person walk? Not very knowingly. That person misses a lot that he or she would like to see and trips over things that he or she can't see. A blind person ends up seeing only his or her failures and lives in a world of darkness. Do you like living in darkness?

When you're self-blinded, you end up feeling sorry for yourself and you punish yourself for the wrong decisions of your life or the mistakes you've made.

When we look at our life introspectively, we cry with Paul, "For the good that I will to do, I do not do; but the evil I will not to do, that I practice. Now if I do what I will not to do, it is no longer I who do it, but sin that dwells in me" (Rom. 7:19-20). We should never let our prayer of introspection be our last prayer.

You go to the doctor when you hurt. Yet the thing that is causing your pain may not be the root problem. The doctor makes a complete examination to find out why you are sick. So, to get well, we have to listen to the doctor and follow his instructions.

He may prescribe medicine or an operation or exercise or other forms of therapy. The point is, we must follow medical advice to get well. In the same way, we must follow the Doctor's spiritual advice to get well.

When you take an introspective journey into your innermost being, you must take the Doctor (God) with you to tell you what is really wrong and what you must really do to get well. Make sure that when you're looking at yourself introspectively, you're looking through God's eyes. Why? Because He is truth and He will tell you the truth.

Always read the Bible when praying introspectively. Then pray with David, "Open my eyes, that I may see wondrous things from Your law" (Ps. 119:18). Then claim the promise, "The entrance of Your words gives light; it gives understanding to the simple" (Ps. 119:130).

God will reveal to us the things we need to know about ourselves, and He will hide what we shouldn't see. God will not show you all your wickedness; none of us could take it. Notice Paul's frustration when he really saw himself:

For what I am doing, I do not understand. For what I will to do, that I do not practice; but what I hate, that I do. If, then, I do what I will not to do, I agree with the law that it is good. But now, it is no longer I who do it, but sin that dwells in me (Rom. 7:15-17).

The prayer of introspection should bring us to the place of forgiveness. When we look away from our sins and failure to Jesus Christ, we seek cleansing.

But if we walk in the light as He is in the light, we have fellowship with one another, and the blood of Jesus Christ His Son cleanses us from all sin. If we say that we have no sin, we deceive ourselves, and the truth is not in us. If we confess our sins, He is faithful and just to forgive us our sins and to cleanse us from all unrighteousness. If we say that we have not sinned, we make Him a liar, and His word is not in us (1 John 1:7-10).

So what can you learn from the above verses? You can learn that when you walk in the light, you are automatically cleansed from *all* sin (see v. 7). God loves to forgive you because He knows you can't live a perfect life; you have a sin nature (see v. 8). He knows you will continue to practice sins (both ignorantly and volitionally; see v. 10). He offers forgiveness if you confess your sins (see v. 9).

Forgiveness is a new beginning, because God allows you to start over again. You can't ignore the sin you find from your *prayer of introspection*. Deal with it honestly—in the desert—and it will amaze you how quickly you find yourself out of the desert and back on praying ground.

However, you must turn away from your frustration and failure. You must learn about yourself and seek His will. Everything you learn about yourself in the desert will be a foundation upon which you can build for the future.

My Time to Pray

Lord, sometimes it feels good when I begin my introspection,
but it feels so frustrating when I stay there.

Lord, I know that in myself is no good thing; I look to You in
Scripture to find the perfect will for my life.

Lord, I confess my sin of self-pity and ask for Your cleansing
and forgiveness by the blood of Christ.

Lord, I will walk the straight and narrow path to fulfill
Your will for my life. Amen.

My Answers Today

_____
_____
_____
_____
_____
_____
_____
_____
_____
_____
_____
_____
_____

For suggested recipes, see pages 180-192.

❧ DAY 18 ❧

Resting in Prayer

*Then Esther told them to reply to Mordecai: "Go, gather all the Jews who
are present in Shushan, and fast for me; neither eat nor drink for three
days, night or day. My maids and I will fast likewise. And so I will go to
the king, which is against the law; and if I perish, I perish!"*

ESTHER 4:15-16

There are many different ways to pray. There are desperate prayers,
warfare prayers, struggling prayers, bold prayers and "never give
up" prayers. But also, there is a time *to rest in prayer*, or silent
prayers. Didn't David say, "I wait quietly before God, for my hope
is in him" (Ps. 62:5, *NLT*)?

If you are fasting from food, you are letting your body rest.
That means your stomach is resting and the heart is not working
as hard to digest your food. Don't forget about your soul. It also
needs some rest.

You begin your Christian life by getting rest from sin. Jesus invited us, "Come to me, all of you who are weary and carry heavy
burdens, and I will give you rest. Take my yoke upon you. Let me
teach you, because I am humble and gentle at heart, and you will
find rest for your souls" (Matt. 11:28-29, *NLT*). After salvation, you
must continue to get stronger spiritually by seeking occasional rest.

Why Silence?

We love noise. Think of all the constant noise within your life.
When I was a young man, we had only three channels on TV; now

there are hundreds available to us. Every time I walked through an airport, I was looking for a pay phone; now I've got a cell phone in my pocket to talk anytime and almost any place. Some people keep their Bluetooth® headset hanging on their ear for ease and increased conversation. I thought that I was up-to-date when I bought an MP3 for constant music. Now the young people Twitter and carry iPhones and iPods. We can get streaming noise without stop.

What did Paul mean, "Aspire to lead a quiet life" (1 Thess. 4:11)? What did God mean, "In quietness and confidence shall be your strength" (Isa. 30:15)? There is power in silence before God. It's not the absence of words that gives us strength; it's God's presence that empowers us. David wrote, "Truly my soul silently waits for God; From Him comes my salvation" (Ps. 62:1). This probably didn't mean original salvation from sin, but our daily salvation from the domination of sin.

We don't learn as much when we're talking as when we're listening. So we need to kneel quietly in God's presence to learn some of the better lessons in life.

Also, we get strength from being quiet in God's presence. Just as our tired physical muscles need rest to regain their strength, so our tired souls need rest to regain determination and courage to work for God. Your stomach is now resting in this Daniel Fast; what about the rest of your physical body? What about your soul?

You can communicate with God in silence. Most people think silence is wasted time because nothing is happening. But does communication happen only with talking? No! Think of two people in love; they can sit for the longest time, looking into one another's eyes, with no sound from their mouths. Yet they are communicating, even when they don't say a word. Their presence with one another communicates love.

But that type of love has to grow in understanding, acceptance and relationship. There's that word again—prayer is *relationship*. Do you have a relationship with God that allows you to sit silently in His presence without talking? Have you received the strength that comes from wordless prayers?

Rest in God

God considers rest so important that He decreed one day out of every seven was a day of rest. Note the fourth commandment:

> Remember the Sabbath day, to keep it holy. Six days you shall labor and do all your work, but the seventh day is the Sabbath of the LORD your God. In it you shall do no work: you, nor your son, nor your daughter, nor your male servant, nor your female servant, nor your cattle, nor your stranger who is within your gates (Exod. 20:8-10).

Why did God create a Sabbath day? Because He first rested on the first Sabbath. "Thus the heavens and the earth, and all the host of them, were finished. And on the seventh day God ended His work which He had done, and He rested on the seventh day from all His work which He had done" (Gen. 2:1-2).

Did God need to rest from His work because He was tired? No! God is omnipotent, which means He is all-powerful. He created all things without effort. God was not tired, but He rested. The word "rested" means ended or finished. God finished what He intended to do, then took a day off. He invites you to practice the same thing.

Because God finished and then rested, He invites you to finish each week in His presence, on His day, with His assembly of people. You should rest—or finish—the work of each week in His presence. We don't keep Sunday laws to please God as did the Jews in the Old Testament. We finish our normal week of work to do His spiritual work on the Lord's Day.

If you dismiss the Sabbath as mere legalism, you miss an opportunity to rest in the Lord. Most people who go away on a vacation don't cease activity. They golf, swim, hike or do other activities that can be just as strenuous as during the work year. But recreation is a renewing activity and, in the same way, you need renewing in your spiritual activity when you rest in God.

We must sit silently in God's presence to practice the presence of God. When you learn of Him, you can practice His presence while stuck in the traffic gridlock or while waiting in a long check-out line. What do you do while waiting for your computer to boot up? Do you ever steal a few seconds by going to God's presence?

Wordless praying is both an art and skill, and there's a difference between the two. Remember that "art" is that expression of your inner nature that comes naturally from the heart. Skill is developed through training, practice and repetition. Art is what you naturally are; skill is what you acquire.

So *resting in prayer* comes naturally when you quit talking. However, there is a skill to the discipline of silence so that something is happening in the silence between you and God. You're growing, you're getting closer to God, and you're getting your prayers answered.

The Jews observed the Sabbath (the Hebrew word *shabbath* means "rest") as a symbol of their covenant with God. Because they lived in an agricultural world, and the work on a farm is never done, God told them to take a day off so they could rest. But more than physical rest, it was a day of worship, learning and spiritual exercise.

Look at the word "recreation." It means to re-create our emotional determination or our strength or our mental focus. We cease one type of activity—work—to enter another type of activity—play—to re-create ourselves. Do you need spiritual re-creation? You get it when you come into God's presence.

Life is a song. All week long we sing the laborious music of business pressures. Just as music starts and stops, is fast and slow and plays on our emotions, so too our workweek is filled with pressures, deadlines, production problems and just the pressure to do better. Then on Sunday we enter the fellowship of believers to sing God's song. We sing praises to Him; we sing our worship, "You are worthy, O Lord" (Rev. 4:11). We sing joyfully our testimony of salvation and His grace to us.

We not only sing with others, but we also sing with God. Did you see that? The Bible teaches that God sings: "He celebrates and sings because of you, and he will refresh your life with his love" (Zeph. 3:17, *CEV*). Because you rejoice in God, and He rejoices in you, why don't you learn His song and sing together with God?

As you fast, learn to rest and sing with God. It will rejuvenate your spirit and renew your determination.

In this chapter, we've discussed silence before God. But there comes a time for words. Talk to God intimately, but not about your project; talk to God about Himself. Tell God what you enjoy about your fast. Meditate on the great things He did in creation. Then turn your thoughts to the great things God did in salvation. Finally, end up thanking God for the things He has done in your life.

After you've talked to God awhile, stop talking and listen for His voice. You probably won't hear an audible voice, but you will receive a message in your heart. He will tell you what to do. He may even tell you how to pray or what you ought to be praying about. Use the following questions to make you think on God.

- As you read the Scriptures, what is God saying to you?
- As you meditate on Scriptures, what does God want you to do?
- As you wait in God's presence, how does He want you to pray?
- For what should you pray?
- What has God said to you through your successes?
- What has God said to you through your failures?

As you wait, ask God to reveal His presence to you. Remember the illustration used earlier in this book: *If you worship the Father, He will come to receive your praise.* Worship the Father because "the Father seeks worship" (John 4:23, *ELT*).

Accept what you learn, do what you know. Too often we go to God's Word to analyze what is said so we can know what it means. But knowing is never enough. Knowing is never wrong, but if you don't put God's Word into action, you never get God's blessing in your life. The written Word of God must become the living Word of God in your heart.

My Time to Pray

Lord, forgive me when I do all the talking in Your presence;
I will listen and be quiet. I will learn.

Lord, forgive me for making my prayer request more important than
resting in Your presence and enjoying intimacy with You.

Lord, I will come apart to fellowship with You in Your presence at
a certain time each day.

Lord, give me spiritual strength to pray for my prayer project, and help me
continue asking to the end of my fast. Amen.

My Answers Today

_____
_____
_____
_____
_____
_____
_____
_____
_____
_____
_____
_____
_____
_____

For suggested recipes, see pages 180-192.

❀ DAY 19 ❀

Urgent Prayer

Prayer is reaching out after the unseen; fasting is letting go of
all that is seen and temporal. Fasting helps express, deepen, confirm the resolu-
tion that we are ready to sacrifice anything, even ourselves
to attain what we seek for the kingdom of God.
ANDREW MURRAY

When you pray urgently, it probably means you're praying with all your heart, and you keep praying because you really need an answer. When a friend faces cancer surgery, you pray because there's nothing else you can do.

Urgent prayers come out of a growing need. Urgency of heart produces urgency in prayer. When you know a bill is due at the end of the month, and you don't have the money, there is an urgency to do something. As the end of the month approaches, you feel more and more panic. You ask yourself, *What am I going to do?* You pray urgently and persistently.

Urgent prayers for lingering problems; Desperate prayers for a crisis.

There is a picture in Psalm 42 of a young deer being chased by hunters. The deer is absolutely terrified and is running for its life. Fear motivates us to cry out for help, and we cry from the bottom of our hearts. Fear peels away our pride and excuses. The answer of Psalm 42 is the first step to your urgent prayer. "As the young deer being chased stays long enough for a drink of water in a mountain stream, so my soul pants for God" (Ps. 42:1, *ELT*).

What about desperation? You pray desperately when there is an immediate crisis. Peter was walking on the water toward Jesus. His eyes were fixed on Jesus. Isn't that the way we should walk our Christian life? Then, "But when he saw that the wind was boisterous, he was afraid; and beginning to sink he cried out, saying, 'Lord, save me!'" (Matt. 14:30). He prayed desperately:

"Lord, save me!"

What is a desperate prayer? It's when you can't prepare your heart by asking for forgiveness of any ignorant sins in your life. Nor do you have time to reverently enter His presence. You immediately cry out like David:

"Help, O LORD my God! . . . save me" (Ps. 109:26).

What can we say about desperate prayers? You panic, or you're in a hole with no way out. There's no way out of your problem if God doesn't intervene.

Sometimes you've tried everything, but every door is closed. You've worked hard to get out of a jam, but now the tide is coming in and you're running out of time. Nothing has worked, so now you're desperate.

On the other hand, sometimes a desperate situation hits when you didn't expect it. You're peacefully driving along when a truck seems to come out of nowhere and broadsides you. You're hurt, and your loved one is lying on the ground bleeding. It's an emergency . . . a crisis . . . you need immediate help. So, you cry out to God, *"Now, Lord!"*

Does urgency describe your present state of affairs? You've faced a prayer project, and you've prayed about a need, but nothing has happened yet. Now you're at the end of your Daniel Fast; you're desperate; you have entered the Daniel Fast to touch God so He will answer your prayers. Read on because you'll learn how to pray desperately.

Preparing to Pray Urgently or Desperately

First, get mentally prepared for emergencies. You should have been asking God to prepare you for future emergencies, but now you are there. So even in the middle of this emergency, ask God to prepare you for future times of trials and testings.

Technically, you can't prepare for an emergency, but you can ask God to give you the ability to deal with an emergency when it comes. Ask God to give you peace in the emergency, and then ask God to give you wisdom to react properly in times of crisis.

Part of your preparation is knowing that difficulty will come. My pastor says continually, "There are more hard days than there are good days in the life of the saints of God; just as there are more valleys than there are mountaintops."

Second, memorize verses that point you to God in time of trouble. When an emergency comes, you will not have time to look up Bible references to encourage you. But if they are hidden in your heart, God can bring them to your mind.

- Psalm 27:5: "For in the time of trouble He shall hide me in His pavilion; in the secret place of His tabernacle He shall hide me; He shall set me high upon a rock."

- Psalm 34:6: "This poor man cried out, and the Lord heard him, and saved him out of all his troubles."

- Psalm 46:1: "God is our refuge and strength, a very present help in trouble."

- Psalm 56:3: "Whenever I am afraid, I will trust in You."

- Psalm 121:1-2: "I will lift up my eyes to the hills—from whence comes my help? My help comes from the Lord, who made heaven and earth."

- 2 Chronicles 14:11: "Lord, it is nothing for You to help, whether with many or with those who have no power; help us, O Lord our God, for we rest on You, and in Your name we go against this multitude. O Lord, You are our God; do not let man prevail against You!"

Third, know when to move from urgent prayers to desperate prayers. You pray urgently for a project because it is a spiritual need. But then a deadline approaches (the end of a Daniel Fast with no answer in sight). Your prayers move from urgency to desperation. You cry out, *"Lord, do it now!"*

When you're hungry, you sit at a table and eat in a civilized way. You use utensils and chew with your mouth closed. But look at the starving person. It's acceptable to gulp and swallow. A starving appetite trumps decorum and polite manners.

So remember, there is a proper time for desperately crying out to God with tears and deep passion.

Fourth, jump right into your prayers. Don't think about what you are going to pray—just pray. Don't consult your prayer lists; also, don't think about how you will frame your request; just pray. Don't get ready to pray—just pray.

If you were cutting weeds in the backyard and a snake bit you on the leg, you wouldn't ask how the snake got there, nor would you question what people will say. You would yell, "HELP!" and run for help.

If you have a desperate situation, open your heart and yell, "Help, Lord!"

Fifth, keep your scheduled times of prayer. As you approach emergencies, you will cry out instantly and wholeheartedly. When a problem comes, immediately lay the problem at God's feet.

But don't let an emergency rob you of your foundation of continuing prayer. As you continue in your Daniel Fast, don't forget about all the other problems in your life and in the lives of your friends and relatives. Keep bringing those before your Father in heaven.

If you have been missing one or two meals a day to pray, then keep that schedule. Remember, it's in those scheduled times of prayer that you find strength. You will need continuing strength in times of crisis, so be faithful in your committed times of prayer.

It's all right for a starving man to grab any food that's close to him. In the same way, it's all right for a desperate person to cry out in desperate prayers. But there comes a time when the starving person returns to normal life. Then he must eat a balanced diet to keep his strength. He must discipline his meal times and meal intake and eat a balanced diet to remain strong. In the same way, a well-balanced prayer life will keep you strong in Christ. Constant, balanced prayer is the best foundation to get desperate prayers answered.

Sixth, bring God into the crisis. King Asa went into battle with 580,000 of his troops against the Ethiopians who had a million men and 300 chariots. The prospect of victory was slight, and the hope of God's people was dark. Asa prayed for God to be with him.

"Asa cried out . . . 'LORD, it is nothing for You to help, whether with many or with those who have no power; help us, O LORD our God, for we rest on You, and in Your name we go against this multitude. O LORD, You are our God; do not let man prevail against You!'" (2 Chron. 14:11).

Did you see what Asa said in his prayers? The Ethiopians were attacking God's people, but Asa realized they were attacking God. Note that he prayed, "Do not let man prevail against You!"

You are fasting and praying for a spiritual victory. Make sure the fast goal is God's project and not your personal project. Sometimes we try to talk God into blessing the project we do for Him. While doing projects for God is good, there is something better. It's when God assigns you a project. It's His project. When you pray, make sure you and God are on the same side.

The emphasis is not on your begging God to come help you win this battle. No, that's the wrong emphasis. It's not even getting God on your side; it's you getting on God's side.

When the prayer project of this Daniel Fast is God's goal, then you can pray with confidence because God will complete His project, in His way, at His time.

My Time to Pray

Lord, I lay this prayer project at Your feet. This is what You have laid upon my heart. I will fast and pray until the end of my vow.

Lord, I have been praying urgently about the prayer goal. Now I come praying desperately for an answer.

Lord, give me faith to believe You for this prayer goal. "I believe, help Thou my unbelief."

Lord, I need Your help now! Amen.

My Answers Today

_____

_____

_____

_____

_____

_____

_____

_____

_____

_____

_____

_____

For suggested recipes, see pages 180-192.

❧ DAY 20 ❧

Spiritual Warfare Prayer

If you are serious enough about the personal and social tasks before you as a Christian to take up the discipline of fasting, you can expect resistance, interference and opposition. Plan for it, insofar as you are able. Do not be caught unawares. Remember that you are attempting to advance in your spiritual journey and to gain ground for the Kingdom. That necessitates taking ground away from the enemy—and no great movement of the Holy Spirit goes unchallenged by the enemy.

ELMER L. TOWNS

I was in Haiti on New Year's Eve when we celebrated the arrival of 1978. I was sleeping on the back screened porch of missionary Bob Turnbull. There is a tremendous amount of demonic activity in Haiti, and New Year's Eve is the high time for satanic manifestation.

I was awakened at midnight when all the church bells in Port-au-Prince began chiming, and the boat whistles in the harbor began sounding and the automobile horns began honking. I was told that at midnight on New Year's Eve, evil manifested itself greater then than at any other time in the year. I shuddered when I became aware of an evil presence on the porch with me.

When in spiritual warfare—because of an evil presence—I pray out loud the name of Jesus and claim His blood for protection. I call on the power of the cross for safety. (Because Satan or demons can't read your mind, you must pray out loud the things you want them to hear.) Then in the darkness of midnight, I began singing out loud songs about the blood of Jesus.

What can wash away my sin?
  Nothing but the blood of Jesus.
What can make me whole again?
  Nothing but the blood of Jesus.

Oh! precious is the flow
  That makes me white as snow;
No other fount I know,
  Nothing but the blood of Jesus.[1]

I got tremendous confidence singing about the blood of Jesus Christ, and it focused me on Jesus, away from any evil that was present. Then I began to ask myself, "What's another song about the blood of Jesus?"

There is a fountain filled with blood
  Drawn from Emmanuel's veins;
And sinners plunged beneath that flood
  Lose all their guilty stains.

Lose all their guilty stains,
  Lose all their guilty stains;
And sinners plunged beneath that flood
  Lose all their guilty stains.[2]

I sang for a long time, forgetting where I was and forgetting my immediate problem. In my mind I went back to the cross where Jesus died for me. In my heart I worshiped the Lord. Then I began to sing again:

When I survey the wondrous cross
  On which the Prince of glory died,
My richest gain I count but loss,
  And pour contempt on all my pride.
Forbid it, Lord, that I should boast,
  Save in the death of Christ my God!

All the vain things that charm me most,
I sacrifice them to His blood.[3]

There's another place in Scripture where we can learn the principles of spiritual warfare. Moses stood on a high hill to see a battle line unfold before him. God's people were being attacked by Amalek—an evil nation that fought against Israel for 1,000 years.

This was not a battle between two nomadic desert tribes, nor was it sword against sword or brute strength against brute strength. It was God against Satan: the kingdom of light against the kingdom of darkness.

As long as Moses held up his arms in intercession to God, the soldiers of God won the battle. But the battle continued throughout the day. When Moses dropped his arms in fatigue, Amalek prevailed. "And so it was, when Moses held up his hand, that Israel prevailed; and when he let down his hand, Amalek prevailed" (Exod. 17:11).

Of course, upheld arms are not a magical way to get a victory. They are like extended hands today as a symbol of our uplifted hearts to God. When God's people face a spiritual battle, they can claim victory by lifting hands and heart to God.

While you are on a Daniel Fast, you'll be tempted like never before, probably because you're attempting to do something you've never done before. You're fasting and praying for 10 or 21 days for a faith project.

So you may encounter (1) a temptation to quit, or (2) have difficulty keeping your mind on God when you should be praying, or (3) you'll think of a past satisfying sin, or (4) a spirit of discouragement will overcome you, or (5) a besetting sin may return, or (6) other un-Christlike attitudes will manifest themselves.

So, most of your spiritual warfare will not be with extremely evil things such as casting out a demon or dealing with supernatural manifestations of demonic power, or obvious anti-Christian people attacking you or your ministry.[4]

Israel's battle with Amalek was a renewal of hostility. The Jews fought Amalek over water rights in the desert much earlier. When

Moses led the multitude to the oasis at Horeb, the people expected water. But the water had dried up. The thirstier the people became, the angrier they complained. Moses cried to the Lord, "What shall I do with this people?" (Exod. 17:4).

God told Moses, "Behold, I will stand before you there on the rock in Horeb; and you shall strike the rock, and water will come out of it, that the people may drink" (Exod. 17:6).

When Moses obeyed, water gushed from the rock. The people understood this was a supernatural victory: "Is the LORD among us or not?" (Exod. 17:7).

Water is more precious than gold to a person thirsting to death. So the Amalekites attacked Israel to get the water rights. There is a principle here: When we have a great spiritual victory, look out! The enemy may be preparing a counterattack.

Perhaps you experienced a great victory by getting many people to agree on a spiritual challenge to a Daniel Fast and pray for a faith project. But remember, getting a group to begin fasting and praying together is only the beginning. Perhaps you feel a personal victory because you've kept your fast for almost 21 days. Watch out! Evil Amalek may be preparing an attack to stop you from reaching a successful end to the fast.

Practical Helps in Spiritual Warfare

Get strength from your friends. The battle in Exodus 17 was not won by one individual. It took Joshua, the general, and soldiers to fight. It took Moses, the intercessor, and Aaron, his brother, and Hur, his brother-in-law, to support Moses' arms. In the same way, remember that there are others who are interceding with you for the faith project. Call on them to pray for your special need. Share with them your burden. Have them pray *for* you as they pray *with* you. "For we are God's fellow workers" (1 Cor. 3:9).

Actively battle against your distractions/temptation. Perhaps you shouldn't close your eyes when praying. But when you keep them open, be careful not to look at things that will also distract your mind. Write out your prayers as you pray them. Underline or highlight your prayer requests as you pray them.

Pray out loud so you can focus on the target. When you are actively putting words together, your mind will not wander.

Change your prayer posture. Just as Moses got tired (because he was old), so your muscles will not hold up indefinitely. Move from kneeling to standing to walking to lying prostrate before the Lord. Keeping the body active may keep the mind focused.

Know your weakest area. The enemy knows your weaknesses and will attempt to attack you there. So don't let him get you there. Write down what is your weakest area, be aware of it, pray about it and be mindful of it.

Pray against your enemy. Some call this "rebuking Satan, or rebuking the enemy." When you pray against the enemy, do so with caution; for our enemy has great supernatural power. But on the other hand, be encouraged; Jesus said, "All authority has been given to Me in heaven and on earth" (Matt. 28:18). Remember the illustration at the beginning of this chapter? I prayed out loud, claiming the power of the blood of Christ to defeat the enemy.

When Michael the Archangel was in warfare prayer, as recorded in Jude 9, he was careful not to pray in self-confidence or to trust his own ability. His response to evil power was, "The Lord rebuke you!"

Be ready for a counterattack against any success you have in prayer. Paul reminds us, "Pray without ceasing" (1 Thess. 5:17).

Claim the victory that is already yours. God has promised, "He who is in you is greater than he who is in the world" (1 John 4:4).

My Time to Pray

Lord, I want to be strong in Your strength; help my weakness and keep me vigilant.

Lord, the Bible says, "I can do all things through Christ who strengthens me," so I yield my weakness to Your strength.

Lord, thank You for every victory I've had in the past; I learn from them and go forward "from victory to victory." Amen.

My Answers Today

_____
_____
_____
_____
_____
_____
_____
_____
_____
_____
_____
_____
_____
_____
_____
_____
_____
_____

Notes

1. Robert Lowry, "Nothing but the Blood of Jesus." http://www.subversiveinfluence.com/wordpress/?p=1433 (accessed December 11, 2008).
2. William Cowper, "There Is a Fountain Filled with Blood." http://www.cyberhymnal.org/htm/t/f/tfountfb.htm (accessed December 11, 2008).
3. Isaac Watts, "When I Survey the Wondrous Cross." http://www.cyberhymnal.org/htm/w/h/e/whenisur.htm (accessed December 11, 2008).
4. Elmer Towns, "The Esther Fast," _Fasting for Spiritual Breakthrough_ (Ventura, CA: Regal Books, 1996), pp. 157-171.

For suggested recipes, see pages 180-192.

❦ DAY 21 ❦

Stay in the Moment

*Fasting is a principle that God intended for everyone to be able to enjoy.
It's not a punishment; it's a privilege! By making fasting a way of life,
you can get closer to God and grow in your spiritual walk like never before.
Fasting is one of the most powerful weapons God has given us for our daily lives.
Through fasting, you can experience a release from the bondage of sin . . .
restoration in your relationships . . . financial blessings . . .
spiritual renewal . . . supernatural healing and so much more!
Another reward of fasting has to do with your future. God has given you
a vision, a divine dream for your life. When you fast, you open up
the blessings and opportunities He has provided for you to pursue that dream.
As you fast, pray for God's direction and guidance. Focus your faith on your
dream and God will show you how you can turn your vision into a reality.
Begin pursuing your divine dream today and make the rewards of
fasting part of your lifestyle.*

JENTEZEN FRANKLIN
(HTTP://WWW.JENTEZENFRANKLIN.ORG/FASTING/)

The Israelites and Philistines were involved in continual warfare, but the Philistines had gained the upper hand by controlling the pass at Micmash (see 1 Sam. 14:1-52). Saul was king, but he did nothing about the enemy; he sat on the outskirts of Gibeah, quite a distance away (see 1 Sam. 14:2).

His son Jonathan devised a courageous plan to defeat the enemy. He decided to climb the cliffs near the pass and fight the enemy. His attack was a tipping point in the battle, and eventually gave Israel the victory. Jonathan created a daring plan of attack.

Jonathan began his strategy by putting his trust in God. He told his armor bearer, "Perhaps the LORD will work for us" (1 Sam. 14:6, *NASB*). Why is it that so many do the opposite; they think, *Perhaps God won't work on my behalf* or *I won't do anything foolish*. Why is it that we are afraid to put God on the spot?

Jonathan's strategy eventually became the vision of all the soldiers of Israel, and they won a great battle. So, as you continue to fast—to the last day—your faithfulness and prayers may motivate others to continue to be faithful in prayer. Together, all of you can win a victory. "Now thanks be to God who always leads us in triumph in Christ" (2 Cor. 2:14).

Your fast vow is not just a dream; your fast becomes an *enabler* because it has motivated you to continual prayer. You, in turn, want to motivate God to act in your behalf.

Perhaps you've been thinking, *If I pray long enough and hard enough, God might do something in this matter.* So, apply the words of Jonathan: "Perhaps the LORD will work for us" (1 Sam. 14:6, *NASB*).

Jonathan's eyes were not on his ability, nor on the fact that he was fighting alone. He knew the number of people fighting wasn't the condition of victory when he said, "For nothing restrains the LORD from saving by many or by few" (1 Sam. 14:6). He knew that he could win in God's power, even though he was only one fighting against many. So, it's not your ability to pray, nor is it your ability to fast that will get answers to your prayer. Look to God's ability to perform what you ask.

Can you see Jonathan climbing cliffs, fighting one Philistine soldier after another, coming to the end of the day exhausted yet victorious? It took repeated steps of faith by Jonathan to gain victory, and he gave everything he had to get it.

But where was Jonathan's father, Saul? He was the king. Saul should have been leading the army into battle. Saul was sitting on the outskirts of Gibeah doing nothing. Are you a Jonathan, or a Saul? If you don't do anything, nothing is going to happen.

Sometimes it seems like the victory is too big and the enemy is too large. The Philistines had high ground that is usually necessary in attacking the enemy. The odds were against Jonathan; yet with God on his side (or rather, Jonathan got on God's side), Jonathan led God's people to victory.

I don't know how long Jonathan surveyed the situation, and I don't know how long it took him to develop a battle plan, but there comes a time when you must go beyond vision to action. There comes a time when you have to go public to tell everyone that you are fasting for a faith project.

But look what happened when Jonathan went public. His armor bearer joined Jonathan's plan to climb the cliff and defeat the Philistines. Instead of laughing at Jonathan, or refusing to go, the armor bearer said, "I am with you, according to your heart" (1 Sam. 14:7).

So there are people in your church or friends within your acquaintances who want to do something for God. But perhaps they're waiting on you to be the "Jonathan." Perhaps they are waiting on your vision. Perhaps they are waiting on you to go public with the challenge; therefore, you need to get them involved in fasting and prayer for the faith goal.

So make a faith statement to move the mountain barrier. Don't be afraid to tell others why you are fasting and why you are praying for the faith project.

One more thing: You'll never be completely ready to pray for 10 or 21 days. It may be that praying for 10 or 21 days is more than you've ever done before. Maybe you've never had experience in fasting. Maybe you think you don't have education enough, or spirituality enough, or enough of anything. But one person—like Jonathan—can lead many others to win a victory for God. What was the result? "So the LORD saved Israel that day" (1 Sam. 14:23).

Don't quit your fast when you're almost to the end. Remember, quitters never win and there are no great stories about people who quit. There's nothing like crossing the finish line with the inner confidence that you've done what you set out to do.

Keep true to your original commitment and be focused on the moment. Do one day's assignment at a time—live within the moment—one day at a time and always with focus on the goal.

To get a college education, you do one day's assignment at a time, attend the classes of that day and pass one exam at a time. Being faithful to your daily assignment leads to a successful semester. Then two semesters add up to a year. Stay in the moment for each day of the second year and you'll have two successful years under your belt. You're halfway there. Continue the process and you'll finish four years of college. But the secret is to make each moment successful.

You never win a race with only a fast start from the starting block. A race is one stride at a time, so learn to remain in the moment and be faithful till the goal is reached.

No one writes a whole book in one sitting; he or she writes one page at a time. No one wins the World Series in the first game of the season; it's winning one game at a time throughout the summer. No one wins the golf tournament with one tremendous shot, so they must focus on the present shot. They must stay in the moment.

Victory is a choice; it's the present pitch of the baseball, the present class you must take, the present stride in the race. Today is the twenty-first day of your Daniel Fast, so stay in the moment. Then later today, you'll reach your goal.

Victory is a door; you must open and walk through the door to enter the victor's circle.

My Time to Pray

Lord, I'm almost to the goal; I will keep my eyes focused on the finish line until I get there.

Lord, raise up a hedge of protection (see John 1:9) around me so that no emergencies or attacks from the Evil One can stop me from reaching the finish line.

Lord, I'm still praying for the faith project for which I'm fasting and praying. Give us the thing for which we fast.

Lord, I give You the credit for enabling me to finish this fast. Now I pray You will be glorified when others hear of this fast. Amen.

My Answers Today

_____
_____
_____
_____
_____
_____
_____
_____
_____
_____
_____
_____
_____
_____

For suggested recipes, see pages 180-192.

❧ SECTION 3 ❧

Appendices

It was in 1994 that the Lord really began to deal with me about fasting in a fresh and powerful way, and to give me new insights into the subject. On July 5 of that year, God led me to begin a 40-day fast for a great spiritual awakening in America and for the fulfillment of the Great Commission throughout the world. Also, on the twenty-ninth day of my fast, as I was reading God's Word, I was impressed to send letters to Christian leaders throughout America and to invite them to Orlando, Florida, to fast and pray together for revival and the fulfillment of the Great Commission. Invitations were soon in the mail. I was praying and hoping for at least "Gideon's 300" to respond positively and to join me at the planned December event. More than 600 came! They represented a significant part of the Christian leadership of America from many different denominations, churches and ministries. It was three wonderful days of fasting, prayer, confession and unity. Many of the leaders gave testimony that it was one of the greatest spiritual experiences of their lives. But before God comes in revival power, the Holy Spirit will call millions of Christians to repent, fast and pray in the spirit of 2 Chronicles 7:14. I have been impressed to pray that God will call at least 2 million Christians to fast and pray for 40 days for the coming great revival.

WILLIAM R. BRIGHT

❧ APPENDIX A ❧

Nine Kinds of Fasts Found in Scripture[1]

To better illustrate and reveal the significance of the nine biblical reasons for fasting, I have chosen nine biblical characters whose lives personified the literal or figurative theme of each of the nine aspects of fasting highlighted in Isaiah 58:6-8. Each fast has a different name, accomplishes a different purpose and follows a different prescription.

I do not want to suggest that the nine fasts are the only kinds of fasts available to the believer, or that they are totally separate from each other. Nor do I want to suggest that there is only one type of fast for a particular problem. These suggested fasts are models to use and adjust to your own particular needs and desires as you seek to grow closer to God. What follows is a brief overview of the nine fasts that are found in *Fasting for Spiritual Breakthrough*.

1. The Disciple's Fast

Purpose: "To loose the bands of wickedness" (Isa. 58:6)—freeing ourselves and others from addictions to sin.

Key Verse: "This kind goeth not out but by prayer and fasting" (Matt. 17:21, *KJV*).

Background: Jesus cast out a demon from a boy whom the disciples had failed to help. Apparently they had not taken seriously enough the way Satan had his claws set in the youth. The implication is that Jesus' disciples could have performed this exorcism had they been willing to undergo the discipline of fasting. Modern disciples also often make light of "besetting sins" that could be cast out if we were serious enough to take part in such a self-denying practice as fasting—hence the term "Disciple's Fast."

2. The Ezra Fast

Purpose: To "undo the heavy burdens" (Isa. 58:6)—to solve problems, inviting the Holy Spirit's aid in lifting loads and overcoming barriers that keep us and our loved ones from walking joyfully with the Lord.

Key Verse: "So we fasted and entreated our God for this, and He answered our prayer" (Ezra 8:23).

Background: Ezra the priest was charged with returning to Jerusalem to restore the Law of Moses among the Jews as they rebuilt the holy city of Jerusalem by permission of Artaxerxes, king of Persia, where God's people had been held captive. Despite this permission, Israel's enemies opposed them. Burdened with embarrassment about having to ask the Persian king for an army to protect them, Ezra fasted and prayed for protection.

3. The Samuel Fast

Purpose: "To let the oppressed [physically and spiritually] go free" (Isa. 58:6)—for revival and soul-winning, to identify with people everywhere enslaved literally or by sin, and to pray to be used of God to bring people out of the kingdom of darkness and into God's marvelous light.

Key Verse: "So they gathered together at Mizpah, drew water, and poured it out before the LORD. And they fasted that day, and said there, 'We have sinned against the LORD'" (1 Sam. 7:6).

Background: Samuel led God's people in a fast to celebrate the return of the Ark of the Covenant from its captivity by the Philistines, and to pray that Israel might be delivered from the sin that allowed the Ark to be captured in the first place.

4. The Elijah Fast

Purpose. "[To] break every yoke" (Isa. 58:6)—conquering the mental and emotional problems or habits that would control our lives.

Key Verse: "He himself went a day's journey into the wilderness. . . . He arose and ate and drank; and he went in the strength of that food forty days and forty nights" (1 Kings 19:4,8).

Background: Although Scripture does not call this a formal "fast," Elijah deliberately went without food when he fled from Queen Jezebel's threat to kill him. After this self-imposed abstinence, God sent an angel to minister to Elijah in the wilderness.

5. The Widow's Fast

Purpose: "To share [our] bread with the hungry" and to care for the poor (Isa. 58:7)—to meet the humanitarian needs of others.

Key Verse: "The jar of flour was not used up and the jug of oil did not run dry, in keeping with the word of the LORD spoken by Elijah" (1 Kings 17:16, *NIV*).

Background: God sent the hungry prophet Elijah to a poor, starving widow—ironically, so the widow could provide food for Elijah. Just as Elijah's presence resulted in food for the widow of Zarephath, so presenting ourselves before God in prayer and fasting can provide for humanitarian needs today.

6. The Saint Paul Fast

Purpose: To allow God's "light [to] break forth like the morning" (Isa. 58:8)—bringing clearer perspective and insight as we make crucial decisions.

Key Verse: "And he [Saul, or Paul] was three days without sight, and neither ate nor drank" (Acts 9:9).

Background: Saul of Tarsus, who became known as Paul after his conversion to Christ, was struck blind by the Lord as he was persecuting Christians. He not only was without literal sight, but he also had no clue about what direction his life was to take. After going without food and praying for three days, Ananias, a Christian, visited Paul, and both Paul's eyesight and his vision of the future were restored.

7. The Daniel Fast

Purpose: So "thine health shall spring forth" (Isa. 58:8, *KJV*)—to gain a healthier life or for healing.

Key Verse: "Daniel purposed in his heart that he would not defile himself with the portion of the king's delicacies, nor with the wine which he drank" (Dan. 1:8).

Background: Daniel and his three fellow Hebrew captives demonstrated in Babylonian captivity that by abstaining themselves from pagan foods, and eating healthy foods, they could become more healthful than others in the king's court.

8. The John the Baptist Fast

Purpose: That "your righteousness shall go before you" (Isa. 58:8)—that our testimonies and influence for Jesus will be enhanced before others.

Key Verse: "He shall be great in the sight of the Lord, and shall drink neither wine nor strong drink" (Luke 1:15, *KJV*).

Background: John the Baptist, the forerunner of Jesus, kept the Nazirite vow that required him to "fast" from, or avoid, wine and strong drink. His fast was part of John's adopted lifestyle that testified to others that he was set apart for a special mission.

9. The Esther Fast

Purpose: That "the glory of the LORD" will protect us from the evil one (see Isa. 58:8).

Key Verse: " 'Fast for me ... [and] my maids and I will fast ... and so I will go to the king' ... [and] she found favor in his sight" (Esther 4:16; 5:2).

Background: Queen Esther, a Jewess in a pagan court, risked her life to save her people from threatened destruction by Haman, the prime minister. Prior to appearing before King Xerxes to petition him to save the Jews, Esther, her attendants and her cousin Mordecai all fasted to appeal to God for His protection.

Note
1. Elmer Towns, *Fasting for Spiritual Breakthrough* (Ventura, CA: Regal Books, 1996), pp. 20-23. To order the book, contact Regal Books (www.regalbooks.com) or phone 1-800-4-GOSPEL.

Six Ways to Fast

There are nine biblical fasts described in *Fasting for Spiritual Breakthrough*. There are nine Bible studies that tell the various ways that fasting was done in Scripture, and the various purposes for which people fasted. However, there are probably as many ways to fast in our modern times as there are ways to pray—obviously, there is no set number in either case. The following six ways of fasting are good guidelines for you to follow or modify as God directs.

1. The *normal fast* or *juice fast* is going without food for a definite period during which you ingest only liquids (water and/or juice). The duration can be 1 day, 3 days, 1 week, 1 month or 40 days. Extreme care should be taken with longer fasts, which should only be attempted after medical advice from your physician.

2. The absolute fast allows no food or water at all, and should be short. Moses fasted for 40 days; but this would kill anyone without supernatural intervention and should never be attempted today. No one should attempt an absolute fast for longer than three days. A person will die if they go longer than seven days without water. The average body is 55 percent to 80 percent water, and must be replenished on a regular basis. Be sure to test the spirit that tries to talk you into a 40-day fast that does not include liquids.

3. The *Daniel Fast*, also called a *partial fast*, omits certain foods or is on a schedule that includes limited eating. It may consist of

omitting one meal a day. Eating only fresh vegetables for several days is also a good partial fast. Elijah practiced partial fasts at least twice. John the Baptist, and Daniel with his three friends are other examples of those who participated in partial fasts. People who have hypoglycemia or other diseases might consider this kind of fast.

4. A *rotational fast*, also called a *Mayo Clinic fast*, consists of eating or omitting certain families of foods for designated periods. For example, a person has an absolute fast for one day to cleanse his bodily system. Then for the next week, he eats food from only one food group or food family. The various food families are rotated to determine what illness may be attributed to certain families of food.

5. The *John Wesley Fast* was practiced by Wesley, the founder of Methodism, prior to the Methodist Conference where the ministries gathered for retreat, revival and preparation for continual ministry. Wesley and the other leaders fasted 10 days prior to the conferences with only bread and water to prepare themselves spiritually so they could teach the pastors.

6. *Supernatural fast.* Moses fasted for 40 days: "He [Moses] was there with the LORD forty days and forty nights; he neither ate bread nor drank water" (Exod. 34:28); apparently Moses spent two 40-day fasts on the mountain praying and receiving the Commandments from God. The two fasts were separated by a few days when the people made the golden calf, i.e., a false God (see Deut. 9:9,18,25). God did a supernatural miracle for Moses in these fasts where a person normally dies when they go without water for more than 7 days. No one should attempt a 40-day fast without water.[1]

Note

1. Elmer Towns, *Fasting for Spiritual Breakthrough* (Ventura, CA: Regal Books, 1996), pp. 23-24. To order the book, contact Regal Books (www.regalbooks.com) or phone 1-800-4-GOSPEL.

❧ APPENDIX C ❧

Recipes to Use During a Daniel Fast

John P. Perkins
Executive Chef and Development Director of the
John M. and Vera Mae Perkins Foundation

When you are focusing on your Daniel Fast and purposing in your heart to give up meat as your sacrifice, you will need to make sure that you are getting enough protein in your diet. You only need 15 percent protein in your diet, and there are a few ways that you can get this necessary amount. One way is by eating legumes, and for this reason eating peas and beans will be important during your fast. In the following section, I will provide you with a few recipes that you can use to infuse the necessary amount of legumes into your diet during your fast.

The Hoppin' John (Black-eyed Peas)
1 lb. dried, soaked or frozen black-eyed peas or field peas
1 large onion, diced small
1 small tomato, diced
½ gallon vegetable stock
½ lb. or 1 cup cut okra, fresh or frozen
salt and pepper, to taste

Bring ½ gallon of vegetable stock to a boil and add peas and onions. Allow it to simmer for 1 hour and 15 minutes. Add tomato after peas have been cooking for 45 minutes. Season with salt and pepper to taste, add a ½ cup of okra, and cook for another 15 minutes. Serve with 1¼ cups white rice (simmer white rice in 4 cups water for 18 to 20 minutes, or cook parboiled rice for 10 to 12 minutes).

Classic Red Beans and Rice

1 lb. dried kidney beans or red beans
1 large onion, diced small
2 bell peppers, diced small
2 tbsp. minced garlic
½ stalk of celery, diced small
¼ cup Worcestershire sauce
¼ cup brown sugar
½ gallon water or vegetable stock
salt and pepper or seasoning salt, to taste

Bring ingredients to a boil and simmer for 1 hour and 20 minutes. Add salt and pepper or seasoning salt to taste and simmer for another 15 minutes. Serve with 1¼ cups white rice (simmer white rice in 4 cups water for 18 to 20 minutes, or cook parboiled rice for 10 to 12 minutes).

Black Bean Soup

1 lb. black beans, dried and soaked
1 small onion, diced small
2 bell peppers, diced small
2 tbsp. minced garlic
½ stalk of celery, diced small
1 tomato, diced small
1 tbsp. olive oil
1 tsp. Italian seasoning
½ tsp. cumin
2½ quarts water or vegetable stock
salt and pepper or seasoning salt, to taste

Sauté the onion, bell peppers, garlic, celery and tomato in a little olive oil until they are translucent. Add mixture to the black beans and water or vegetable stock and your Italian seasoning and cumin. Bring to a boil and then allow the beans to simmer together for 1 hour and 20 minutes. Add salt and pepper or seasoning salt to taste and simmer for another 15 minutes.

Homemade Granola

2½ oz. sesame seeds
2½ oz. sliced almonds or pecans
11 oz. oats
4 oz. cashews
4 oz. honey
3 oz. dried cranberries or raisins

Toast the sesame seeds in a dry skillet until golden brown. Place in a separate bowl. In the same skillet, toast almonds or pecans to a pale golden color. Add the sesame seeds and continue to toast until the nuts are golden brown. Add the oats and cashews to the skillet and continue to toast, stirring until light brown. Add the toasted sesame seeds and honey to the skillet. Heat and toss until all the ingredients are coated with the honey. Remove the pan from the heat and stir in the cranberries or raisins. Spread mixture on a baking pan with a liner of parchment paper at the bottom. Bake in an oven at 350° until golden brown (about 15 minutes). Allow the granola to cool and then break into chucks. Store in a cool dry place. (**Note:** Unlike many other cereals, oats retain the majority of their nutritional elements after the hulling process. If you eat this recipe in moderation, it will be a considerably enjoyable snack—but it is high in fat, so watch your intake.)

Fresh Fruit Parfait with Honey-Vanilla Yogurt

1 qt. nonfat vanilla yogurt
4 oz. honey
8 oz. banana, diced
6 oz. strawberries
5 oz. apples, cooked
8 oz. granola
sprig of mint (if desired)

This recipe is a great compliment to the above granola recipe, and when accompanied with fruit, you can't beat this dish. Begin by stirring the honey into the vanilla yogurt. Place fruit in a separate bowl and toss together; keep refrigerated until needed. Place a small layer of granola in a presentation dish, wine glass or parfait cup. Place a small layer of yogurt over the granola, and then place a small layer of fruit (bananas, strawberries and cooked apples) over the yogurt. Continue this pattern until the dish is filled. Garnish with the granola and add a sprig of mint if desired.

Daniel's Vegetable Fajitas
2 tbsp. olive oil
1 tbsp. garlic
5 oz. red onions
12 oz. red bell pepper
12 oz. yellow bell pepper
12 oz. green bell pepper
1 lb. shredded cabbage
12 oz. cooked kidney beans
5 oz. red chili sauce
18 flour tortillas

Heat the olive oil in a large sauté pan. Add the onions and the garlic. Sweat the onions until they are translucent. Add the peppers and cabbage and sauté until tender (add a teaspoon of water if necessary to sauté the cabbage—the cabbage cooks by steam). Stir in the kidney beans and chili sauce and heat just until warmed. Cover the tortillas with a lightly damp towel in a warm oven at 225°. Wrap vegetable mixture in the warmed tortillas. (**Note:** I often select this recipe because it is healthy, and those who enjoy Mexican cuisine will particularly enjoy it. Bell peppers are a great source of vitamin A, B and C and contain folic acid, which expecting mothers especially need during their pregnancy.)

Grilled Vegetables
12 oz. yellow squash, sliced about a quarter-inch thick on an angle
10 oz. zucchini, sliced a quarter-inch thick on an angle
6 oz. yellow or red onions, sliced a quarter-inch thick
6 oz. green bell pepper, sliced a half-inch thick

6 oz. red bell peppers, sliced a half-inch thick
6 oz. medium mushrooms, sliced in half
5 oz. balsamic vinaigrette

For this recipe, you will need to get out your grill. Grilling is one of my favorite things to do as a chef, and vegetables taste so good when they are grilled. For this recipe, first toss all the vegetables in balsamic vinaigrette (as a marinade) for about 30 minutes. Then grill the vegetables on a gas grill or a flattop grill for 2 minutes on each side (fork tender). You can also add eggplant, tomatoes and other veggies.

Wild Rice Succotash

1 tbsp. extra-virgin olive oil
6 oz. whole corn kernels
5 oz. medium mushrooms, sliced
2 tomatoes, diced
4 oz. butter peas or lima beans
4-6 oz. wild rice or white rice (cooked)
2 oz. vegetable stock
1½ oz. scallions, sliced thin on an angle

Heat the olive oil in a sauté pan. Add the corn and mushrooms and sauté until tender. Add the tomatoes, peas or lima beans, rice, vegetable stock, scallions and salt and pepper to taste. Mix the ingredients and heat thoroughly. (**Note:** Cooking with corn, mushrooms, tomatoes, butter peas or lima beans and wild rice is a great combination. This is a leftover type of dish that can turn corn or rice used in a previous meal into a succotash. Every mother in the world needs this recipe!)

Roasted Corn and Black Beans

1 tsp. of olive oil
1½ oz. red onions, diced
2 garlic cloves, minced
1 lb. roasted corn kernels

6 oz. dried black beans, cooked
1 tomato, diced
1 tbsp. lemon juice
salt and pepper, to taste
2 tbsp. chopped parsley
1 tbsp. chopped cilantro

Heat the olive oil in a large pot. Add the onions and garlic and sauté until translucent. Add the corn, beans, tomato, lemon juice and salt and pepper to taste. Toss over high heat until the mixture is hot. Remove from the heat and stir in the cilantro and parsley. (Note: This dish is versatile and makes a great side, but it can also be very filling as an entrée.)

Barley Pilaf
5 oz. onions, diced
1 tbsp. garlic, chopped
1 qt. vegetable stock
11 oz. barley
2 bay leaves
1 tbsp. Italian seasoning

In a saucepan, sweat the onions and garlic in 2 ounces of the vegetable stock until the onions are translucent. Add the barley, bay leaves, Italian seasoning and the rest of the vegetable stock. Bring the liquid to a boil and cover the pot tightly. Cook in an oven at 350° for 45 minutes or on a stove 12 to 15 minutes until the pilaf has absorbed all the liquid and the barley is tender. Stir in herbs just before serving. (Note: You can turn this into a Barley Walnut Pilaf by adding 2 ounces of chopped, toasted walnuts to the pilaf before the barley is cooked. After the barley is cooked, add another 2 ounces of chopped nuts.)

Basic Rice Pilaf
6 oz. of yellow onions, diced
4 oz. celery

2 tbsp. vegetable solids (margarine)
16 oz. white rice
30 fl. oz. vegetable stock or water
6 oz. broccoli florets
8 oz. baby carrots
salt and pepper, to taste

Sweat the onions and celery in 1 tablespoon margarine until they become translucent. Add the rice and sauté with the onions and celery. Add the vegetable stock or water to the rice mixture. Cook rice in the oven at 350° for 40 minutes or on top of the stove until rice is tender but not finished cooking (about 12 to 15 minutes). Add the broccoli and carrots and continue to heat until the rice and vegetables are cooked all the way through. Add 1 tablespoon margarine and salt and pepper to taste. (**Note:** This is my southern variation of the classical French dish Rice Pilaf along with the Barley Pilaf recipe that I presented to you earlier. Both are outstanding dishes and deserve to be in your repertoire.)

Stir Fried Barley
4 oz. green bell pepper, diced
2 oz. onion or shallots, diced
2 oz. carrots, diced
2 oz. celery, diced
2½ tbsp. olive oil
16 oz. barley pilaf
½ tsp. dried thyme or 2 tsp. fresh thyme

In a saucepan, sweat the peppers, onions, carrots and celery in the olive oil until tender. Add the barley pilaf and thyme and stir-fry until heated thoroughly. (**Note:** This is my favorite type of recipe for this particular fast. It is a compound from a previous Barley Pilaf recipe. These are the type of recipes that enable you to use leftovers, keep a low-food cost, and save money in the end. Dieting is expensive, and we have to be good stewards of our resources.)

Rosti Potatoes with Celeriac

20 oz. russet potatoes
20 oz. celeriac
1 tbsp. Dijon mustard
½ tsp. Cavenger's Greek Seasoning
1½ tbsp. olive oil

Peel and grate the potatoes and celeriac. Combine the grated potatoes and celeriac, mustard and seasoning. Form the mixture into 20 1½-oz. cakes or 10 3-oz. cakes. Heat enough oil to lightly coat a nonstick sauté pan. Sauté the cakes until golden brown on each side. Finish by cooking the cakes in the oven at 475° until thoroughly heated (about five minutes).

Daniel's Four-Grain Waffles

1 qt. nonfat buttermilk
3 whole eggs
2 oz. vegetable oil
8 oz. all-purpose flour
6 oz. whole-wheat flour
6 oz. rolled oats
3 oz. cornmeal
2 tbsp. baking powder
2 oz. sugar
9 egg whites

Combine buttermilk, whole eggs and vegetable oil in a large bowl. Combine all dry ingredients (flours, rolled oats, cornmeal, baking powder and sugar) in a separate bowl. Add the dry ingredients to the liquid ingredients and mix just until incorporated. Whip the egg whites to a soft peak and fold into the batter. Lightly spray a hot waffle iron with vegetable oil. Ladle the batter into the waffle iron and cook until the waffles are golden brown (about 3 minutes). Serve immediately. (**Note:** topped with the fruit salsa below, this is wonderful treat for the fast.)

Barley and Wheat Berry Pilau (Pilaf)

3 oz. wheat berries

15 oz. vegetable stock

2 tsp. vegetable solids (margarine)

1 oz. leek, diced

2 oz. carrots

½ oz. celeriac, diced

2 tsp. of minced shallots or red onions

2 tsp. minced garlic

6 oz. pearl barley

5 oz. white grape juice

salt and pepper, to taste

6 oz. chopped spinach

Soak the wheat berries for 8 to 10 hours in 3 times their volume in water. Drain the berries and combine with the vegetable stock. Cover and simmer until tender (about 1 hour). Drain any excess stock and reserve. Heat the margarine in a medium saucepan. Add leeks, carrots, celeriac, garlic and shallots or red onions. Sweat until the vegetables are tender. Add the barley, grape juice, salt and pepper and the reserved wheat berry cooking liquid. Bring the liquid to a boil and cover the pot tightly. Cook in an oven at 325° or on the stove until the barley is tender and has absorbed all the liquid (about 45 minutes). Cook the spinach in lightly salted water until tender. Drain well. Combine the wheat berries, barley and spinach and serve.

Vegetable Pot Pie

1 lb. frozen mixed vegetables

6 oz. whole kernel corn

6 oz. broccoli florets

13½ oz. cream of celery soup

2 pie shells (one deep dish)

This recipe has the potential to become a family favorite. Combine the mixed vegetables, corn, broccoli florets and cream of celery soup in a bowl. Mix together and place in the deep-dish pie shell. Invert the other pie shell, place on top of the pie filling, and crimp the sides together. Place slits on the top pie shell, creating vents for the vegetables to steam and the shell to cook properly. Place in the oven at 365° for 50 minutes. Serve with cranberry sauce.

Vegetarian Dirty Rice

3 oz. dried cranberry beans
2 oz. onions, diced
2 garlic cloves, minced
14 oz. vegetable stock
7 oz. long-grain rice
1 tbsp. tomato paste
1 tbsp. vinegar
2 tbsp. minced roasted jalapeño
1 tsp. crushed black peppercorn
1 tsp. Cavenger's Greek Seasoning
1 tsp. pepper
1 tsp. paprika
¼ tsp. cayenne
3 oz. grated cheddar cheese
4 oz. roasted corn kernels

This powerful dish is one for the ages and will go along well with your fast. First, cook the cranberry beans in boiling water until tender. Drain and mash with a fork and keep as reserve. In a medium saucepan, sweat the onions and garlic in 2 tablespoons of the stock until they turn translucent. Add the rice and sauté briefly. Add the remaining stock, tomato paste, vinegar, jalapeño, Cavenger's Greek Seasoning, pepper, paprika and cayenne. Bring the stock to a boil and cover the pot. Cook in an oven at 350° until the rice is tender and has absorbed all the liquid (about 18 minutes). Fold the mashed beans, cheese and corn into the rice.

Vegetable Burgers

1 lb. carrots, grated
2 oz. celery, grated

2 oz. onion, grated

1 oz. red pepper, minced

4 oz. white mushrooms, minced

4 oz. scallions (green onions), minced

4 oz. walnuts, minced

1 egg, beaten

½ tsp. parsley, chopped

½ tsp. thyme, chopped

1 tsp. minced garlic

1 tsp. salt

½ tsp. Tabasco sauce

½ tsp. sesame oil

¼ tsp. ground black pepper

1 oz. crackers, crushed into meal

I couldn't have written the recipes for this fast without our giving you a burger to eat. There are a lot of veggie burgers out there—the only difference is that this one is good! First, place the carrots, celery, onion and pepper into a sieve, and press to release the excess liquid. Place the mixture in a large bowl and add the mushrooms, scallions, walnuts, egg, parsley, thyme, garlic, salt, Tabasco sauce, sesame oil and black pepper. Stir to thoroughly combine. Add enough cracker meal to make a firm mixture, and form into 10 3½-oz. patties. Roll each patty in additional cracker meal if desired. Bake each patty on a sheet pan lined with parchment paper at 475° until thoroughly cooked (about 10 minutes).

Wild Mushroom Chowder

2 tsp. vegetable solids (margarine)

4 oz. onions, diced

2 oz. celery

1 tbs. minced garlic

1 oz. arrowroot or cornstarch

1 qt. vegetable stock

12 oz. russet potatoes, peeled and diced

6 oz. evaporated skim milk

2 tsp. heavy cream
2 oz. grape juice
1 lb. wild mushrooms (without the stems)
5 oz. mushroom stock
salt and pepper, to taste

You can't go wrong with this soup! Begin by heating the margarine in a large soup pot. Add the onions, celery and garlic. Sweat until tender. Combine the arrowroot or cornstarch with enough stock to form a slurry. Add the remaining stock to the vegetables and bring to a simmer. Add the slurry to the stock and bring to a simmer until thickened. Add the potatoes to the thickened stock and simmer until tender (about 15 minutes). Remove the pot from the heat and add the evaporated milk, cream, grape juice, salt and pepper. In a large sauté pan, sweat the mushrooms in the mushroom stock until tender. Gently stir into the soup and enjoy.

Tropical Fruit Salsa
16 oz. mango, trimmed and diced small
8 oz. papaya, trimmed and diced small
4 oz. red bell pepper, diced small
4 oz. red onion, diced small
4 tbsp. cilantro
4 tbsp. lemon juice
1 tbsp. minced jalapeño
2 tsp. olive oil
salt and pepper, to taste

Combine all ingredients and allow to set for one hour before serving (refrigerate if not serving immediately). (**Note:** To prepare this dish for a dessert or brunch item, substitute mint for the cilantro, strawberries for the peppers, and onions and honey for the olive oil. Serve as a filling for crepes or with muffins, pancakes or French toast, or accompany with biscuits. You can also substitute honeydew melon, cantaloupe and pineapple in place of the papaya and mango to create this dish.)

Black Bean and Corn Loaf

2 tbsp. corn oil
6 oz. onions, diced
6 oz. red pepper, diced
2 oz. minced garlic
12 oz. cooked black beans
4 oz. seasoned tomatoes
2½ tbsp. cilantro, chopped
¼ tsp. Tabasco sauce
1 qt. vegetable stock
1 tsp. salt
½ tsp. crushed peppercorns
8 oz. cornmeal
2 oz. all-purpose flour

Heat the corn oil in a large skillet. Add the onions, red pepper and garlic and sweat until the onions are translucent. Remove from the heat and stir in the beans, tomatoes, cilantro, and Tabasco sauce. Heat the vegetable stock, salt and peppercorns in a saucepan. Slowly whisk in the cornmeal. Reduce the heat and simmer, stirring constantly, until the mixture pulls away from the sides of the pot (about 20 minutes). Remove from the heat and fold the beans mixture into the cornmeal. Lightly spray a 1½-quart loaf pan with vegetable oil and place the mixture in the pan. Refrigerate for 8 to 10 hours. When ready, unmold the loaf and slice into 15 equal slices. Slice each piece on the diagonal to make 30 triangles. Lightly dust 2 triangles for each serving and sauté in a hot skillet sprayed with oil until golden brown.